WALDEN III

WALDEN III

IN SEARCH OF A UTOPIAN NIRVANA

STEPHEN WOLINSKY, PHD

DEDICATION

To Avadhut Nityananda;
   beyond the realm of consciousness
To Sri Nisargadatta Maharaj;
   prior to consciousness
To Sakyamuni Buddha
To Nagarjuna

SPECIAL DEDICATION
TO THE GREAT PHILOSOPHERS

Jacques Derrida
David Hume
Ferdinand de Saussure
Baruch (Benedict) Spinoza
Ludwig Wittgenstein

and, In Memory of My Father, Harold Wolinsky

ACKNOWLEDGMENTS

My divine Leani forever
Tara Hopkins (word processor)
Gregory Sawin (editor of this book;
   and Vice President of Publications
   of the International Society
   for General Semantics)

TABLE OF CONTENTS

GETTING STARTED

When "I" was at Ohio State University, "I" was a psychology major, and "I" was a poor student. In those days, being a child of the late 60s, most of us were interested more in everything from Vietnam, politics, having sex, taking drugs and, for "me" personally, psychology. In 1971, "I" was finishing college and thinking about going to graduate school, and trying to face the question of where should "I" go, and what university would even take someone with such a poor grade point average. "I" met with one of the psychology professors because "I" needed a letter of recommendation. He asked "me"; "What are your plans, what are your thoughts, what is it you would like to do?" Very spontaneously out of "my" mouth, came this idea, "I would like to write *Walden III*." (Around 1854, we had *Walden* by Henry David Thoreau, and about 100 years later we had *Walden II* by B.F. Skinner, the novel about a society or commune based on principles of behavior modification, which gave rewards and punishments to shape the desired behavior.) Even then, more than 30 years ago, I had no idea about what shape *Walden III* would take. However this fascinated "me," my boldness in thinking that "I" could write such a thing as *Walden*

III, but also my certainty that that is what "I" would do. In about 1992, "I" had tried my hand at writing a novel called *Walden III*, and in Boston, while teaching a workshop, "I" even went to Walden Pond for some thought or inspiration. Well, the novel went nowhere. It was submitted to Bantam Publishing House, and it was given a polite rejection. "I" realized that "I" really did not have the talent, nor the skill, to write a novel as the vehicle for conveying what "I" wanted be convey in that genre.

The idea of writing *Walden III* did not arise again until the latter part of 2001. The question was how to organize such a book to convey the message "I" wanted to present. "My" new idea was "Well, why don't we just have dialogues," dialogues between some "**Teacher**" and the great philosophers, ranging from Socrates and Plato to Descartes in the West, and to somehow include both Buddha and even Confucius in the East. In this way we could discuss the "great" and not-so-great ideas and philosophies and theologies of the West, and even include Martin Luther, Saint Augustine, and the Christians along with psychological theorists. But the idea of a dialogue somehow seemed too similar to the question-and-answer (Satsang) books that were circulating all over the world.

At the same time "I" began to realize that this was a perfect genre, not only for "me," but also for conveying certain "understandings." "I" reviewed *Plato's Republic*, a book containing dialogues between the "great" Socrates and people who had come into *dialogue* with him. In Buddhism (the Buddha lived in about the same time period), much of the early material was in the form of *dialogues*. Questions and answers were exchanged between the students and the "master": in this case, Buddha and some disciple, or in the case of Socrates, either a student or an adversary, i.e., someone who had an opposing point of view or a point of view that Socrates would dismantle through a series of very simple questions (the Socratic Method). Moreover, in India's most famous text, the *Bhagavad Gita*, Arjuna (the unenlightened student) presents his questions to Krishna (the enlightened master).

Not to overstate, this genre was not used only by people going to a "**Teacher**" in the East, but also in the West. In the 1700s, the great Scottish philosopher, David Hume, wrote a book on religion. In this book, the man of great wisdom was called, under a fictitious name, Philo (who, of course, was David Hume), or in Nietzsche's *Thus Spoke Zarathustra* (of course, Zarathustra had to be Nietzsche).

In this genre, and with this understanding, we can begin to embark on this tour of some principal *discourses*[1] and systems where great philosophers meet with the "**Teacher**" to look at, question, discern, and explore exactly what these concepts mean and what is their impact on "life."

"I" began to appreciate that there was a genre for this approach. The problem "I" noticed was that *almost*

---

[1] Discourse: All that is written or spoken and all that invites dialogue and conversation. Discourse and *langue* (Saussure) ventriloquize us, because it is prior to the arising of words thought, and the "I." We imagine we are thinking. Rather, the discourse tells us what we imagine we think. The thought and the "I" is produced from the discourse before we realize it. Discourse is *not* a product of the "I," rather it produces the subjective "I" experience, which later gets translated as a narrative story one tells oneself. In this way it has a constituent role in the production of symbolic systems that govern human existence.

all of the books of this type over the last 50 years, questions placed before the "**Teacher**" were for the most part very superficial. Questions were so superficial that unfortunately they never really evoked or produced the depths of the "knowledge" that these "**Teachers**" *might* have had. And for that reason "I" found that most of the question-and-answer books were boring.

For that reason "I" began to come up with the idea that in order to get answers to the *big questions*, or get the "real stuff," we had to have the right questions asked by the right questioner. It was essential to have people meeting with the "**Teacher**," people who could ask the *big questions* and someone who could answer those *big questions*. In this way, not only did the questions have to be good, but the questioner had to have "thought" things out in great depth "within themselves" in advance, as Socrates or Plato did. These are the questions that needed to be answered, because not only had the philosophies, the belief systems, the lenses, the frames of reference been thought out, but these great philosophies were the vehicles for structural seed stories or metaphors we live by (see Glossary or footnote for *discourse, discursive structure, structural*). In this way, we would be questioning not only a philosophy, but questioning an archetypal-mythological seed story, which some anthropologists consider as 1) early indigenous science; 2) early indigenous cultural explanations and/or stories to justify social roles, systems and rituals, which have been accepted as true and real, yet are unproved fables; or 3) stories to resolve life's contradictions, 4) stories to warn people of catastrophies, or 5) explanations about how we got here.

The structural seed stories and metaphors that are

proposed are what Western and Eastern belief systems are organized around. In short, language, speech, and culture are one and the same, and structural seed stories, once fertilized, watered, and ritualized, then grow and sprout into relational, cultural, emotional, moral, psychological, and religious rituals, which seem rational, and yet go unquestioned.

In the East (India, for example), much is attributed to the metaphor or structural seed story of reincarnation, and in Western Christian cultures, the structural seed stories of Heaven and Hell. And so, underlying all of these are the major concepts and systems that organize cultures in every area in Europe, Asia and the United States. For example, on Sunday, nobody works, it is somehow God's day, even though few believe that God created the world and rested on the seventh day.

REVIEW

In this way, this dialogue approach views the questioner's importance, because the questioner represents the "famous" voice of some kind of underlying belief system, metaphor, archetype of understanding or seed story. Later this was dropped as "I" began to understand that the famous "person" who imagined that he came up with the theory or story *was not* important, but rather the speaker was the mouthpiece for a discourse, a perceiver who was telling this story (philosophy), which, as it happened, later became culturally and linguistically adapted and spread like a seed.

In other words, the discourse-structure ventriloquizes us and makes Plato "famous." But he is not the author of the discourse, the discourse authors him; as noted philosopher Michel Foucault suggests, the discourse produces the philosophy, not the other way around (philosophy provokes the discourse). In short, all of us are products of our discursive structures[2].

WHY THE TITLE, WALDEN III: IN SEARCH OF A UTOPIAN NIRVANA?

The title, *Walden III*, was chosen to suggest *Walden*, that "external" or "internal" utopian Nirvana, which so many of us seek. The subtitle, *In Search of a Utopian Nirvana* emphasizes the seeking for the "place-space" of a heavenly utopia. Nirvana essentially implies (incorrectly, as we will discuss later) that piece of Heaven, or a state of consciousness. The expression, *in search of* explores that from the "beginning" of self consciousness, when "you" realize that "you are," or "I am," you went *in search of an identity*; being a good child or a bad child; *in search of*, "What should 'I' say?"; *in search of*, "What should 'I' not say?"; *in search of*, "Who should 'I' be?"; *in search of*, "Who should 'I' not be?"; *in search of*, "Who should 'I' model myself after?"; *in search of*, "Who should 'I' not model myself after?" etc. Even as you grow older, there are certain rules, norms, standards, and societal rituals that society places on you, with some of the most disgusting words, such as the expression, *be realistic. Be realistic* translates as "see the

---

[2] Discursive structures are the products of discourses. It determines the role of the subject. Discourses refer to knowledge about objects. They do not have authors and are constituted by arch(ives) or an anonymous collection of texts or language. In this way the discursive structure determines what we think; the discursive discourse ventriloquizes us—*we* (the "I" we imagine ourselves to be) are echoes of the *discourse*, not the other way around.

world the way I see it," or *common sense*, which translates as the bourgeoisie status quo, or *appropriate*, which really means "what fits into the rules and game structures contained within each particular society." A game structure is a system suggesting that you behave, think, act, and live in a certain way, which is central or at the center of society. If you do not behave, think, or act in this way, then you are *marginalized*, diagnosed, and somehow unacceptable. These implicit structures Michel Foucault calls discourse or a *discursive structure*. This discursive structure predates "I" consciousness and underlies not only what we think, but what it is OK to think, do, or say. The discursive structure fits you into a particular model, or a particular identity of what you're supposed to be, not only in terms of actions and behavior, but also in terms of where you should be in your life; how you should look, act, behave and even think.

This underlying drive or *will to create an identity*, this *will to find the right way of behaving, being, doing, and having* is survival based. Later in life it becomes sublimated and justified as a lifestyle. This or any structure insists that somehow, if "I" do the right thing, "I" will be able to reach or have some kind of *utopian Nirvana*. In this way, the will (drive) to survive becomes the driving force to try to create or have an identity that will take you to Nirvana.

This is painful because, in the socialization process that we all suffered through so terribly, we are asked to conform to certain actions, behaviors, ways of moving, etc., in short, endless game structures, societal rituals, and rules that are not questioned. They become so automatic and driven by survival that, as years go by, these substructures yield thoughts, feelings, emotions, behaviors, etc., which continue because they are just assumed to be right. For example, you don't say what you feel; rather, you phrase it a certain way. You don't just yell and say you're angry; you have to say, "Now I need to discuss something with you." And certainly the pain of socialization and fitting in; *in the search for identity*, which allows you to fit in; makes people feel like a piece of meat being run through a meat grinder, with society hoping that all the pieces come out *docile* and the same. The pain of this process is overwhelming. Unfortunately this process is duplicated later in the *search for* or *in search of a utopian Nirvana*.

Moreover, what will be discussed throughout this book is that <u>the "I" is a by-product of these structures, and the "I" does not exist separate from them. The self is a conglomeration of structures.</u> *AND there is no self that is separate from these structures*!!!

The Bourgeois Seeker

To the European readers, the word *bourgeois* is very common. "I" first came across the word *bourgeois* when "I" was 15 years old; I was reading Karl Marx's *The Communist Manifesto*, and later "I" wrote a paper on Marx's dialectical materialism. So, let me define *bourgeois*, even though many readers might already know what that means. A *bourgeois* person is a very middle-class person whose main goal and desire is to become comfortable, normal, they "take on" and internalize cultural rituals (psychological and spiritual) and standards to fit in; and they want to have some status. They do not want to rock the boat. They do not want to create problems. They are just trying to find a way to be comfortable and normal in their lives; hence, they become *docile.* To illustrate, "I" know a man in Massachusetts who is involved in spirituality and psychology, and is a professional psychotherapist. For the most part, he is interested in comfort, and just wants to fit in. For this reason he *docilizes* himself and in the name of helping his clients, he *docilizes* them. He calls this *docilizing* "normal" and "appropriate." We could say simply that during the socialization process, our society, religions, schools, etc., attempt to control, socialize, and normalize us. To "docilize" implies the process whereby we internalize this external *docilizer* (society, parents, church, etc.). Another extreme example of the *docilizing* process occurs in the book/film, *One Few Over the Cuckoo's Nest*, in which the main character (played by Jack Nicholson) is helped by Nurse Rachet who lobotomizes him as a way of helping him fit in.

Comfort or Freedom

In order to clarify this desire for comfort over freedom, let us differentiate here between comfort and freedom. In Dostoyevsky's monumental work, *The Brothers Karamazov*, the most interesting piece of that book for "me" is a 20-page segment entitled "The Grand Inquisitor," which is a story within a story that is told by one brother, Ivan, to another, Alyosha. Ivan tells a story about the Spanish Inquisition. It is during the Spanish Inquisition that a cardinal, "The Grand Inquisitor" is responsible for torturing people. Suddenly, Christ appears!! Now, in the first few pages, Christ is arrested and put into prison. In the next 15 pages, the Grand Inquisitor explains to Christ why he must have him killed. Christ has to be killed because people were not interested in freedom; people were interested in being comfortable within their belief system. In this particular case, the Catholic religion gives comfort, but *not freedom.*

"People have been more persuaded than ever that they have perfect freedom, yet they have brought their freedom to God and laid it humbly at our feet. At last (the church) has vanquished freedom and have done so to make men happy."

(Dostoyevsky,
The Brothers Karamazov, p. 260)

I quote Jacques Derrida, the father of postmodern deconstruction: "Do we need to be saved *by* our abstractions,[3] or do we need to be saved *from* our abstractions." "My" vote is that *you need to be saved from your abstractions.* But *bourgeois seekers*, middle-class seekers who are only interested in being comfortable with so-

---

[3] An abstraction in this context refers to the work of Alfred Korzybski who wrote, "We are immersed in a world full of energy manifestations, out of which we abstract directly only a very small portion, these abstractions being already colored by the specific functioning and structure of the nervous system—the abstractors." (Korzybski, *Science and Sanity*, p. 238) This term, *abstraction*, refers to the result of the nervous system and sense organs omitting billions of stimuli and selecting only a fraction, less than 1%. This enables the nervous system to perceive and construct, out of "energy" in motion, an "I"/perceiver. This process of omitting or leaving out, which is performed by the nervous system, is called abstracting; and it is through this process that the "I" is created. An abstraction is a nervous system's "construction" or "creation." The "I," the perceiver, and the perceived are constructions of the nervous system. The result of the abstracting process is called an abstraction, a metaphor; in this case, one abstraction is the "I" (subject) (the perceiver), and other abstractions are the physical world as well as the perceiver's emotional and ideological realities; all of these are constructed out of **NOTHING**.

cietal belief systems, community and/or status, have a tendency to take on different systems, different philosophies, or different lifestyles, in an attempt to make themselves feel comfortable. They do not really want to confront anything. They just want to be comfortable. Now there is no criticism in that. It's just an opportunity for all of us to look at ourselves and ask, "Are we interested in freedom, or are we interested in comfort?" The *bourgeois seekers* are interested in comfort, trying to make their lives as comfortable, normal, and painless as possible. "Don't confront me, let's just feel good." They just want to feel comfortable; they really don't want to look at what's under the structures. To paraphrase the Grand Inquisitor,

> *'They surrender their freedom to us*
> *and serve us as if we can set them free.*
> *We are given reverence and thanks for*
> *bearing the burden of freedom.'*

(Dostoyevsky, *The Brothers Karamazov*)

A real seeker is willing to confront anything. So, before we go into the book, you might want to look at where you are on the continuum: Are you a *bourgeois seeker* or a true seeker interested in freedom.

Who's Who in Heaven?

In 1979, "I" was living in India and "I" had learned the spiritual game (at the time "I" did not know it was a discursive structure). "I" had known who was in charge of the *ashram* where "I" lived; "I" knew "I" had a nice room, and "I" had my nice schedule. We joked because "I" knew all the people there, how to get what "I" wanted, i.e., be comfortable and fit in. We said that we should write a book called *Who's Who in Heaven*. Basically, "I" knew the game structure. When I met Sri Nisargadatta Maharaj ("my **Teacher**") he asked "me" if "I" knew who "I" was. My reply was "I feel a lot of love, I feel a lot of bliss, I can even see energy patterns." He said (with great disgust), "I'm not interested if you're satisfied or if you're pacified with your spiritual life. Do you know who you are?" I said "No." He said, "Until you do, you shut your mouth." What is the significance of that statement in relation to the bourgeois seeker? The bourgeois seeker can go to an ashram, a workshop, a group, a meditation retreat, or join a community and, eventually, *they learn the game structure*. They do not know that it is a game, but they learn how to play the game. They can play the game, they can talk the game, they meet on Sundays and have little chats with their friends, they can go to meditation classes or even teach meditation classes. That's the spiritual game. The bourgeois seeker takes these techniques, tools, attitudes, beliefs and adds them to their life, creating a "spiritualized" patchwork self to make their lives more comfortable. But this does not lead to freedom. A "true seeker" realizes that nothing can be sacred, nothing can be sacrosanct, nothing can be something that you don't look at; rather, they are ready to look at anything, to feel anything, to go through anything, to walk through Hell if necessary to discover who they are. They are not *bourgeois*, or as Karl Marx might call them, *petty bourgeois*. There is no act, there is no appropriate or inappropriate. For that reason, when "I" met Nisargadatta Maharaj, that is what

"I" trusted. He was not a saint in white with a long white beard sitting and pretending to be something he was not. He was not a *simulation* or a conglomeration of all of our images clustered together, which matched what a "**Teacher**" should be or act like. He smoked cigarettes, drank tea, yelled and screamed, did whatever he did. There were no rules, there were no regulations; "he" was what it was. A free person, totally free on every level. He did not play anyone's games, nor did he "take the bait" of adoration or trance-ference. A "true seeker" understands this, a bourgeois seeker fights it. So, when we go through this text, inquire: Are you a bourgeois seeker who has organized their "wonderful" life and just added a new psycho-spiritual activity, but underneath it, are you still a miserable person who maintains a plastic act, or are you a "true seeker"?

"I" remember conducting a workshop in Germany, and one of the big therapy gurus from Holland came to my workshop. He did very well and loved the work. But when asked, "What are you going to do with this work?", his response was, "If I take on this work, I will have to change my entire practice, change my entire business. I will have to change everything; therefore, I will not do it." Another person, who attended my training near Freiburg, Germany, had just completed a long therapy training and had been certified. She said she realized that the training she was just certified in was not it and had many inconsistencies. But she had to make a living; therefore, she would continue to use it and teach it. This is the *bourgeois seeker* turned *bourgeois lying teacher* for two reasons. First, the job of a therapist or "**Teacher**" is to come up with the best technology available to help the client or student. The job of the therapist or "**Teacher**" is not to stay in business in order to keep their practice going, nor is it a popularity contest, nor is it to create an extended family and support trance-ference. Imagine, if you had a heart problem and you went into the hospital for heart surgery, and the heart surgeon said, "I will use this procedure, which isn't as good, because it makes me more money, and you will give me more acknowledgment than this other procedure, which works better, but won't make me much money or make me feel as valuable." How would you feel as a patient? Is this a client-centered or seeker-centered therapy or spiritual practice? Or is it a therapy or spiritual practice for the *bourgeois therapist*, the *bourgeois seeker*, and the *bourgeois teacher*? Until those questions are answered, we'll be stuck in a society of not only *bourgeois seekers, bourgeois teachers, bourgeois therapists*, but we will continue to be stuck with the *bourgeois political system* that just "fakes you out" to get you to believe that somehow if you play this *bourgeois game* and dance this dance, then you too will be comfortable and ultimately you will get to some utopian Nirvana.

Deconstruction

This text aims at the entire deconstruction and annihilation of all structure that binds. It aims at the annihilation, through inquiry, with extreme prejudice, every metaphoric structure that organizes "our" civilization. The *bourgeois seeker, therapist, or teacher* (one who is just interested in their status, feeling that they have some personal value or worth, making money or making a living first; and [possibly even unknowingly] interested in their client or student second) must be annihilated once and for all. In this way, the small number of people who truly *"knew"* all along, can be freed from the fallacy of what Friedrich Nietzsche called *slave virtue* and the *herd mentality* by recognizing that they were stuck in structures and belief systems, which they took on, or were given to them on some level.

Post-Deconstruction

After spending six years in India and studying with the most profound Advaita-Vedanta teacher of the last half century, Nisargadatta Maharaj, "I" got propelled in two ways: 1) the way Advaita-Vedanta and Buddhism in its purest form dismantle all spirituality, philosophy, and psychology; 2) how and what forms of Western philosophy and spirituality as well as Eastern psychology and spirituality would get dismantled by Advaita-Vedanta, Buddhism, bio-physiology, and linguistics; and 3) most importantly, how could the deconstructive process be enhanced, simplified, and clarified. It is not difficult to dismantle much of Eastern and Western philosophy and religion; the question becomes, What, if anything, of East and West is left or is worth keeping? To understand the process, power, and importance of deconstruction, one must appreciate what the *Vedanta* in "Advaita-Vedanta" means; in Sanskrit, **Neti-Neti**, translated means *Not This, Not That*.

In order to appreciate the depth of this, we must realize that the discovery of I AM THAT—YOU ARE NOT, or more (in)accurately described as finding out who you are, "we" must discard (dismantle, deconstruct) everything YOU ARE NOT. What then should be discarded? This can best be answered when we look at the question asked to Nisargadatta Maharaj, "Who are you?" His reply, "Nothing perceivable or conceivable."

This response gives us a peek into **Neti-Neti** or post-deconstructions' deconstruction; namely, discarding everything perceivable and conceivable. Because of this, Nisargadatta Maharaj emphasized that "all that could be taught is understanding; the rest comes on its own."

To transmit this understanding, "I" felt it was critical to include other approaches (some scientific, some "spiritual," some philosophical, and even some linguistic) so that, rather than parroting words, we can deeply understand the depth and power of **Neti-Neti** deconstruction, and hence, a context for this transmission.

The Six Approaches of *Neti-Neti* or Post-Deconstruction

1. Advaita-Vedanta
2. Buddhism
3. Neuroscience
4. Quantum physics
5. Linguistics
6. Western philosophy

Make no mistake, this text explodes the imagined world that most do not know is imaginal. But please, tuck away somewhere in "your" consciousness that purpose of these explosions; or as Yoda (the "**Teacher**") proclaimed in the movie, *Star Wars: Episode V— The Empire Strikes Back*, "You must unlearn that which you have learned," in order to discover who you are, were, and always will be.

In summary, the book will contain sections dedicated to different pieces of what we call theories of reality or structural seed stories, representations[4] of particular lenses from which people view their lives and then deconstructing them. Good luck. See you in the main text.

With Love, Your Brother
Stephen
January, 2002

P.S. "I" know that, oftentimes, "I" do not explore the footnotes. In this text, it is probably a good idea for you to read the footnotes or consult the glossary on page 233; it will make this material clearer down the road.

Stephen

---

[4] This is the result of abstracting. The nervous system *represents* or reproduces through the abstracting process a "picture" of what is. For example, if you look at a tree, your eye-brain system constructs a visual image that *represents* a tree, it is not the tree itself—the "map" is not the "territory." To put it another way, the result of your nervous system abstracting only a small amount of the billions of stimuli (energies of the atomic world) is a visual "map" of the tree in your brain. This visual image is an abstraction; it is the result of your eye-brain system trying to make "sense" out of the chaos of billions of energies impinging on and stimulating your eye-brain system. Therefore, your resulting "sensation" is what we call "tree." However, what you see is only a representation, an abstraction; The tree itself is not in your brain, but your representation (your map) is in your brain. More importantly, the perceiver and the "I" that perceives and draws conclusions, are also abstracted representations produced by the nervous system through abstractions <u>which are made of</u> **NOTHING**. Hence, what you see is a simulation a copy of a copy, of a copy, which has no original, or originary presence or origin.

CHAPTER 1

THERE IS NO WALDEN III

"The history of western metaphysics is a continual search for a logos or an originary presence."

—Jacques Derrida

Why use the title *Walden III*? "I" chose it because there is an impulse, a drive, a will to organize, transcendentalize, and reach metaphorically, Walden. A place or space of origin and presence that is beyond our words, meanings, structures, and the "I" and the experience of life. Let us be clear about this: *There is no utopia, origin, presence, State of Mind, Place or, in a word, Walden. The paradox of Walden III is that there is no Walden III!!* The question then is what is this "will to seek"? Can it be that physiologically, as well as psychically, we are ruled by survival and the searching/seeking mechanism in the brain? And, whether this be true or not, you can notice *that no "I" has ever found Walden!! Why? Because The "I" is not and Walden is not.* This could be as the Buddha said, "You will not necessarily be aware of your own enlightenment."

The *Siva Sutras* were discovered by a 10th Century poet saint underneath a rock in Kashmir. The fourth sutra says that "*the cause of bondage is sound.*" More specifically, the cause of bondage is what is called *matrika shakti*. It is the "energy" which comes out of **NOTH-ING**, which produces sounds, sounds produce letters (Ferdinand de Sassure called this the *langue*[5]), letters produce words, words produce sentences and concepts; but, moreover, these words not only produce concepts, these words produce the "I." <u>*The "I" and all thoughts exist in sound only, and in language only!*</u>

There is no "I" separate from language. Just to illustrate, say out loud the words, "I am happy." Now, think the words, "I am happy," without words or sound. *Thoughts are words.* Thoughts, according to one of the greatest philosophers of the 21st century, Ludwig Wittgenstein, are just sounds that name things. Thoughts and the "I" (thoughts) cannot exist unless there are sounds transduced by the ear-brain system into language and speech.

In the ancient Vedas thousands of years ago, there was a group called the *Grammarians*. Grammarians specifically dealt with language, speech, and sound. Why does this become critical and pivotal to the "understanding"? If concepts, the "I," and differences or similarities exist only because of sounds and they exist in language only, then as Wittgenstein would say, "All of your problems are based in words and sounds." If there were no words, there would be no problems.

---

[5] "The langue refers to the overall system of signs or words (along with its rules of grammar, syntax, and standard usage).... The langue lies deeper than thought and is accepted unconsciously, rather than chosen consciously, by those who use it (in this it shares some similarities with the discursive structure of Foucault." (Dr. Louis Markos).

TO BE OR NOT TO BE. THAT IS THE QUESTION.

The question is, do things actually exist? Let us look at the word *is*. The word *is*, we imagine stands in for, or refers to, the concept of existence. The word *is* gives the illusion of its existence. *Is* is a representation, and every word and sound gives the illusion of not only its existence, but its presence and beingness. This representation suggests a pre-existent presence, essence or beingness of a thing, which is conjoined to the word *is*. For example, there is an illusion, that the **word** *virtue* is a **thing** *called virtue*, which exists somewhere; and the word *virtue* represents this thing, action, or behavior *called virtue. Rather, and this is important, there is no virtue outside of the word "virtue,"* and what culture, society, or religion, decides virtue is.

The Search for Logos

Why is this search for the logos[6] so important? The logos promises to give meaning and purpose to all things and to act as a universal reference point, a transcendental touchstone, an original cause that can always be referred back to. It is this *will* to find an original purpose and an original presence, which drives Western metaphysics, as well as Eastern metaphysics. This is because people want so much to have a universal center, a transcendental ego. But why does all of this happen? All of this is driven by "a desire for a

---

[6] This refers to the ultimate or primal center or presence or transcendental self that existed prior to this world or from which this world came. This center (God) gives meaning and purpose to all things and serves as a comparative reference point against which truth (with a capital *T*) can be determined.

higher reality, a Walden, a utopia, a Nirvana, a Heaven, a full presence that is beyond, and not a part of this world. Plato believed this presence or essence existed prior to what we see. With the understanding or realization that there is no prior presence, no virtue or God outside of the word *God*, this illusion dissolves and "spirituality" collapses as a metaphysical language game[7].

What all of this means is that the human nervous system in its desire to organize chaos, holds the basic assumption that if we can find the universal answer, the original presence, the one that organized all of this, call it God, then all of our problems and everything will be answered and everything will be organized and everything will be okay.

Someone who is organized, *logos centered*, considers that meaning comes ultimately from some original source that is pure and untouched or unaffected by this world (metaphysics comes from meta-beyond and physics, meaning the physical, e.g., beyond the physical). Why is this so significant? This is so significant

---

[7] A way of using signs (words). What words mean is determined by how they are used. Wittgenstein said that usage determines meaning, and there is not a pre-existing mental image, or presence, or essence. Language games (sentence, propositions or truth claims) are tautologies. Lyotard, borrowing Wittgenstein's language games, says that they contain their own rules, and conventions. A *language game* is a system of communication; it is linguistic activity guided by rules. A sentence is a "move" in the game of language; words and sentences are meaningless without the system or structure of which it is a part. Philosophy confuses *language games*, that is, using the words of one language game according to the rules of another language game. Each language game is autonomous. (Glock, *Wittgenstein Dictionary*, pp. 193-196) Therefore, language games are what metaphysics is made of, since the "I" and the metaphysics exist in language only, and there is no "I" or metaphysics outside of language.

because one of the projects of this text is to make clear that everything perceivable or conceivable, including the "I," is an abstraction, a linguistic metaphor.

The problem or pain that we derive from this drive or *search for the experience of a utopian Nirvana* is that 1) words are arbitrary (Ferdinand de Saussure), 2) words have no meaning or presence outside or prior to their use (Ludwig Wittgenstein), and 3) the concept of a center, the concept of an original presence, which organizes everything, exists in language only and, as such, is a representation of a reality that is ultimately nonexistent. Another part of this project is to dismantle (quantum psychology), or deconstruct (post-modernism), this *will* to find the original source or presence, which exists in language only, and then dissolve this painful drive to find that which has no permanent, separate, independent existence (Buddhism). This putting together of different teachings provides us with a peek into **post-deconstruction** (to be discussed later).

For this reason, we will clarify Nisargadatta Maharaj's use of the word *concept*, shifting it to the word *language*. Secondly, we will call metaphysical explanations *language game*s (Wittgenstein). Simply put, the spiritual philosophical search for a utopian Nirvana, either as a place-space, or internal or external, as well as the psychological quest (for a cause that yields Nirvana) or metaphysical explanation, exists in language only, and amounts to a *language game*. *Before* either verbal or nonverbal language, the "I" is not, or as Nisargadatta Maharaj said, "prior to your last thought, stay there." What is Nisargadatta Maharaj's nonverbal *I am*? The nonverbal *I am* is prior to thought, prior to the sense or the verbal *I am*. But it is still an "experience," and as such, it is a representation, which, therefore, "uses" abstracted nonverbal words or sounds. So what are some of the other projects of this text? 1) All problems and the "I" exist in language only. 2) These sounds, which form language, words, letters, "I," and both the concept of existence and nonexistence, exist only at the level of words. 3) Deconstruct basic sounds and *language games* which form letters, which form words, which form concepts, which have organized Western as well as Eastern spirituality and psychology, which we call structural seed stories, so that "we" can get a hint about what, if anything, is left when all this is gone.

The One Substance

To deconstruct is the focus in this **Neti-Neti** or the **post-deconstruction** process. To do this, we will use one concept: Everything is made of *one substance*. Then, at the end of the text, deconstruct the *one substance*.

When we say that everything is made of the same *substance*, what we will *not* say is that *this substance becomes* something other than what it is, because if we said the *one substance* becomes something other than what it is, then we would be forming a polarity and a hierarchy, meaning that this "pure" *substance* could be higher than what it becomes, i.e., God is higher and separate from what it created. We will not go that route. Rather, what we will say is that everything is made out of the same *substance* including the chair, the thought, the idea of hate, the idea of love, the experience of hate, the experience of love, the experience of shit; everything is made the same as *the substance* itself. We will break out of the trap of *polarity*, or in the words of post-modern deconstruction, we will break down the trap of *binaries*, a center, a presence, or a source by saying there is no source, there is no original presence, these exist in language only.

THE EARLY GREEKS:
THE CHANGING—CHANGELESS CONTROVERSY

The roots of the *one substance* and impermanence live not only in Buddhism and Advaita-Vedanta, they began more than 2,500 years ago in Greece with Heraclitus and Parmenides. Heraclitus's most famous saying is, "You never put your foot in the same river twice," meaning that the world is in constant change. To paraphrase Heraclitus, in about 800 B.C., oppositions are unreality. Day and night are one (one thing) in being the same substratum in different states. The unity is more fundamental than the opposites. The opposites are essential features of the unity, but that unity is in constant change. In contrast to the view of Heraclitus is that of Parmenides, also in about the 8th century B.C., who states that there is no change—only *one substance*:

Parmenides and The Way of Truth

Parmenides denies change, and he says this about *the substance*:

A. It is ungenerated. It is not unperishing.

B. A single whole (not divided, indivisible)

C. Unmoving

D. Perfect - balanced – no boundaries.

"Nor is it, nor will it be, because it is one, continuous."

E. Unstarting and unstopping. It never starts nor
stops. Changeless.

(Long, *The Cambridge Guide to Early Greek Philosophy*,
pp. 91 & 96)

This constant change of Heraclitus and the unchanging Parmenides can be reconciled. *As the one substance* there is no change; *as the witness* of the *one substance* there is only change. It should be understood
that although *the substance* "becomes" objects, it never loses its true nature. Just as a necklace, a ring, and a
bracelet are still made of the same gold.

More strikingly, to begin to appreciate **post-deconstruction**, if there is only *the substance*, and everything
is *the substance*, then there is no *substance* and nothing
"*is*" (because the quotation marks around "is" demonstrates that "is" is an abstraction). Appreciating this,
along with other approaches, both scientific and spiritual, we will deconstruct structural discourses and
seed stories, which underlie and organize everything
and everyone in both the Eastern and Western worlds
with the impulse to find an original source or presence.
In this sense, we will use *the substance* of Advaita-Vedanta, the emptiness of Buddhism, the undifferentiated consciousness of Northern Kashmiri Tantra, along
with modern-day neuroscience, philosophy, linguistics, and quantum physics as the context for transmit-
ting this "understanding": Simply stated, in the words
of Roland Barthes, "*we will deconstruct all authority*."

The One Substance as Brahman
and the Early Hindu Grammarians

What part does language play? "Brahman (according to the Vedas) is the word principle. Brahman creates all objects and phenomena in the form of words," itself must be in the nature of words . . . Brahman is sound, all phenomena assume the form of words and also because it manifests as the uttered phonemes (sounds) (Poona, 1969, p. 107). "The word principle is a dynamic entity." (p. 108) "All phonemes are the word principle." (p. 117) "Brahman is the eternal undifferentiated word principle. Brahman as *the substance* is both the pre-word (*sab*, in Sanskrit) as well as the word principle (*dattva, in Sanskrit*) (p. 180).

Why is Language the Problem?

According to Jacques Derrida, the father of postmodern deconstruction, the problem with language and words is that a word and its meaning always refers to or defers to another word and its meaning. If you say to me, "It is raining outside." and I say to you, "What is rain?" You'll say, "Rain is water that comes from the sky." "I" could say, "What is water?" "Water is H_2O." I could say, "What's H_2O?" Moreover, words and their meanings are based on sensory input, which means that words can be based only on abstractions (of some "energies"), and not *directly* (without a participating nervous system) based on the "things" themselves (p. 74).] So we find that all language and all words *refer to* or *defer to* another word. Since all language refers to and defers to another word, and since there is no original origin or presence in language (language and words are abstractions that refer only to other abstractions); then language always defers meaning. In other words, language is an abstraction, and meaning exists only in an abstracted language, not as the thing in itself, we can say. There is no thing up there (metaphorically speaking) called virtue that exists outside of the word *virtue*. Meaning, therefore, is "always already" deferred or postponed. If meaning is "always already" postponed, then the desire to have meaning, to have an original source, to have an original logos, this desire for the logos, is the desire to find meaning in words. But words are abstractions that defer meaning; they refer to other abstracted words or descriptions. Even the word *logos* is a word, a description, an abstraction, which exists in language only. In this way, there is no logos outside of the word *logos*, which we have given meaning to. But the meaning is always deferred to other words, which defer to other words. A logos exists in language only, and the frustration can be that you can never find or have meaning in language. *The "I" and enlightenment exists in language only, and there is no meaning in language.* All meaning is always deferred and postponed for both the "I" and enlightenment, which are concepts, words, which exist in language only. It is for this reason that the "I" cannot be (as it is an abstraction, a representation whose meaning is "always already" deferred), and enlightenment (even as an experience requires an abstracted experiencer— "I"), exists in language only; hence enlightenment can never occur for a "I" because both are abstractions of **NOTHING**. This is a very powerful statement. A major project of this book is to take apart structural seed stories, dismantle them or deconstruct them so "we" can realize *"the substance."* Actually you will never re-alize it, you will *be* it and you won't know it. Why can you not know it? Because it is language that differen-tiates things, and (to greatly paraphrase the Buddha) *it is language that makes things seem as though they have a separate independent individual presence or existence when they do not.*

"You will not even be aware of your own enlightenment."

Buddha

Jacques Derrida, uses the word differance[8] (differ-ance with an *a*) to say this. Language is a system based on differences. For example <u>c</u>at is different from <u>b</u>at, is different from <u>s</u>at, but it is the consonants that make differences and that make language possible. All lan-guage is an abstraction that refers or defers to another word; so if you are looking for meaning (or the thing in itself), you are always stuck in what Derrida calls an *aporia* (Greek for waylessness).

---

[8] Pertaining to a process coined by Derrida, whereby meaning chang-es over time, and ultimately meaning is put off, postponed, or deferred forever. Coined by Derrida, the word functions most importantly on the word *defer*. Meanings are "always already" deferred as they always re-fer to other words. Thus meaning is never reached. This leaves one in an *aporia* (Greek for *wayless*)—in limbo and feeling anxious, because mean-ing can never be reached in language but is "always already" deferred (to other words, which defer to other words). The reference to *"differance"* takes up Saussure's argument that meaning is no more than the product of the differences between signs (words), coupled with a deferral sys-tem, meaning that language provides no stable meaning. Moreover there is no correspondence between signifier (sound) and signified (concept). In Saussure's language, all words are arbitrary. This is central to decon-structing the metaphysical tradition of the logos as the primal word.

To dismantle all of this and realize that language and sound, as the ancient Vedantans, called Grammarians, would have said, is to take language apart and to realize *the substance*. The *substance*, which everything is made of, which *is everything* and, *which is, therefore, no differences*. So, there *is* no deferment prior to language. Ultimately, once this "understanding" is transmitted, language dismantles itself because ultimately what language represents *is not*. This means that *Walden III and Nirvana is not*, because once the *substance* is realized, there is no *substance* or "I" to realize it. Hence, everything is dismantled and *there is no Walden; there is no utopia; there is no Nirvana; and, of course, there is no you*.

There is No "I" Separate from the Discursive Structure of Language

The discursive structure of language produces the "I." This can be seen as the infants pick up the language and discursive structure of their parents, as well as the parents' spiritual beliefs, whose structures act as seed stories sprouting and producing a series of spiritual and psychological *language games*, which are the voice and words of discursive structure.

Poststructuralism or postmodernism[9] deconstructs the structure of the language. Language produces logocentric[10] *language games*, which give the illusion of a transcendental source, origin, or presence beyond

---

[9] Whereas modern theory seeks to invert binaries and set up new structures of thought, postmodernism deconstructs binaries, which tends to privilege one structure or center over another. Moreover, postmodernism deconstructs all logos, center, presence or originary sources.

[10] This is an adjective used to describe systems of thought that claim legitimacy by reference to external, universally true propositions.

the structure of language. This language game hides the structure, and hides the fact that *there is no Walden outside of the word Walden and there is no Nirvana prior to or outside of the word Nirvana. As Buddha said, Nirvana means extinction.*

By deconstructing the structure that is carried by language, whose meaning is both arbitrary and deferred, the "I" centered, logos-centered, ego-centered universe, centered on presence, essence, and origin is "seen" as *aporiaic* (wayless) in nature; hence, it collapses and disappears. This disappearance is *Nirvana as extinction.*

Existence Precedes Essence (Presence)

The most important existential understanding, which began with Nietzsche and later Heidegger and Sartre, was that existence precedes essence. This means there is no essential thing or presence that exists prior to the word existence.

Before the existentialists, Plato believed in an essence, a presence that was transcendental and unaffected by the "I" or language.

Existence precedes essence (presence) is the understanding that there is no presence or essence of things prior to existence (the *I am*), and that there is no transcendental presence prior to existence.

Plato believed, as we will see later, that ideas and things had prior essences. Buddha deconstructs that with, "There is no independent self nature" or Nagarjuna's (Middle Way Buddhism) there is only "dependent arising." Translated, this means there is no presence or present outside of the word presence. And that everything is so connected that there is no separate, in-dependent self, essence, entity or deity; hence "depen-dent arising."

The Six Deconstructive Approaches (Metaphors)

1. Advaita-Vedanta: There is only *one substance*.

2. Neuroscience: The "I"-perceiver arises after the ac-tion and event has already occurred.

3. Buddhism: Form is none other than emptiness, emptiness is none other than form.

4. Quantum Physics: Everything is emptiness. Form is condensed emptiness.

5. Linguistics: The "I" is a metaphor which exists in language only.

6. Western Philosophy (David Hume): Cause and ef-fect are perceptions, which are abstractions.

WALDEN III MADE SIMPLE

1. Nothing exists outside of language.

2. The "I" is a metaphor which exists in language only.

3. Enlightenment exists in language only.

4. A source, origin, ultimate cause, or God exists in language only.

5. All experiences require an experiencer and, as such, are abstractions of **NOTHING**.

6. The process of getting to a source, called a path, is impossible, because the source or originary presence or existence is a linguistic metaphor and an abstracted representation. Hence, source exists in language only; it does not exist outside of the language game, and it is a language game.

7. The meaning of words is dependent upon their usage and relationship to other words. Meaning and the things represented, along with the perceiver, exist in language only; they have no meaning outside of language.

8. The meaning of words is always already deferred or postponed inside of language.

9. Everything you think you are, you are NOT. Why? The "I" exists in language only, and is a metaphor.

10. Stay in the Nothingness "prior" to language.

11. The experiencer is part of the experience; a separate experiencer is a linguistic illusion only.

12. There is only *one substance* that exists in language only and not at all.

13. There is no spiritual outside of the word *spiritual*.

14. There is NO WALDEN utopian Nirvana.

Wolinsky to **Nisargadatta Maharaj**: "I do the so-ham, ham-sa mantra."

Nisargadatta Maharaj to **Wolinsky**: "It means *I am that – that I am*? If I write down 10 pounds of gold on a piece of paper, is it the same as 10 pounds of gold? You must meditate [deconstruct] past your concepts [language]."

The Approach Simplified

1. There is only *one substance*.

2. The nervous system is late. The "I," and the perceiv<u>er</u>, arises after the action has already occurred.

3. All is an abstraction of **NOTHING**, which *appears* in language only, hence the "I," the self, and enlightenment are in language only.

The concept of god was produced in man through natural selection. It was a functional survival benefit to believe so.
Moreover, feelings like love were also naturally selected to enhance survival. In a word they all had a function.

Charles Darwin

CHAPTER 2

WHO'S WHO IN WALDEN III

The Describers of What is Not

Beginning now, and throughout the text, there will be two characters; "*R*" or the recorder, and "*A*" the "**Teacher**" and answer<u>er</u> of the proposed structural seed story (as in the psychic structure constructed of language), seed (as in an idea that sprouts), and story (as in a linguistic narrative). Simply stated, the seed has a structure that manifests and brings forth its fruit in an abstracted language, which forms a story or *language game*. Let us begin this by allowing the "*R*" (recorder) to tell his narrative story.

"I" got chosen to be a recorder, possibly because "I" had spent time with many gurus in India. "I" recorded with a tape recorder, and some notes, exactly what occurred. "*A*" had appeared some 70 years ago and was a very simple man, not a learned man, not a man with an education particularly, but he had "seen" more than something. "He" had seen beyond the metaphor called "mind." For this reason, and during this period of time, there was a series of people that began to appear to question "*A*". These were philosophers, psychologists, teachers from India, teachers from Germany, teachers from Greece, teachers of some renown. Each one seemed to be questioning something. Certainly we can say beyond a doubt, or certainly "I" can from "my personal" perspective, that they were seeking some kind of realization, understanding, way of living, ethics, lifestyle, or some way to understand the human condition. Simply stated, they wanted answers to the **big questions**. "I" feel comfortable in saying that they were seeking some idea or experience of a utopian Nirvana, which they interpreted as some kind of "heaven" or "utopia," some kind of way of living, being, doing, and having that permitted them a level of peace and contentment. All of these great thinkers, philosophers, and teachers were looking for this and (in their own life, when they were honest in their midnight confessions) had hit a stone wall. The stone wall was very simple: Although they worked so hard, tried so hard, did so much in their own fields; although they meditated on, extrapolated, demonstrated, hypothesized, and possibly even had experiences; what was most shocking was that all of them, or should "I" say most of them, had no abiding uninterrupted state or a no-state of peace. This was a great quandary because the principles that these particular people had laid out were principles that had lasted, in some cases in the West and in the East, some 2,500 years or more. "I" recorded not only the sessions on audio tape, but "I" insisted on the publication of the manuscript to include what happened to "me" "inside" "myself" as "I" was sitting in this room with only three to five people, sometimes less, as the deepest questions, the **big questions**, not only the "Who am I?" questions, but also "How do I live my life?" questions, or "What is virtue?" or "What is morality?" or "What happens when you die?" type of questions were asked and answered. "I" also, in my own "insides," put in my "experience" or comments. As you go through the book, you'll notice *structural seed stories* rather than names of the question<u>ers</u>. This is because the person and the "I" are merely a mouthpiece for the structural seed stories, although we have all been taught that this particular person, like Plato, thought it up. Hopefully this will become clearer as we move through the text. "I" will say only that the answer<u>er</u>, the one to whom the questions were directed, was *"A"*.

Signed *"R"*

The whole history of philosophy is nothing but a series of footnotes to Plato.

Alfred North Whitehead

SECTION II

"R"'S OVERVIEW

Getting Us Up to Speed

CHAPTER 3

SOCRATES, PLATO, AND THE LEAP OF FAITH

As the recorder, "I" felt it part of my job to bring the reader up to speed about what will be discussed. "I" thought it was important because it might be difficult for the reader (unless they have some background and understanding of the *who* and the *what* these dialogues are, and where they came from) to appreciate the depth of *"A"* and how these structural seed stories are pivotal.

Socrates was Plato's teacher. He was famous for his Socratic Method. In using this method, you ask questions, you *inquire*. Socrates lived about 2,500 years ago, which makes him a contemporary of the Buddha. In this section we will delve into the "origins" of Western philosophy. Socrates' method was inquiry: "What is (fill in the blank)? People would approach him, with some knowledge they thought they had, he would ask questions about it, and before you knew it, the person was in a state of perplexity, a state of confusion. Some famous questions of this era were, for example, "What is virtue?", "What is justice?" When Socrates asked "What is virtue?" and continuing to ask "What is virtue?", the concept of *virtue* began to dissolve, until the person who believed they were an authority on virtue or an authority on justice, would realize that they didn't really know what they were talking about.

Now, 2,500 years later, in quantum psychology, through the teachings of Sri Nisargadatta Maharaj, the inquiry approach was used once again to take apart, not only "<u>What is</u> virtue?" or "<u>What is</u> justice?", but it also was used to dismantle images, ideas, concepts, or notions that people had about themselves and had about others. At the risk of jumping to the end of the text, later on, when "*A*" encounters one of the great philosophers of the 20th Century, Martin Heidegger; "*A*" will answer Heidegger's lifelong question, "<u>What is being?</u>" or "<u>What is the meaning of being?</u>" In short, to paraphrase "my **Teacher**," Sri Nisargadatta Maharaj, he said that all concepts were frames of reference, lenses, whereby the "I" viewed itself and hence, viewed the world, and they should be discarded.

In this text, "*A*" will clarify this by saying that language creates the "I," and to paraphrase and use the terminology of Ludwig Wittgenstein, all concepts form and are *language game*s, and concepts exist in language only.

SOCRATES, PLATO, AND THE WEST

Some of what came out of the ancient Greek civilization was an inquiry into how we can live a good life. There was this *search of, this search for* an identity, *a search for* a way of being, or *a search of* how to be, in short an inquiry: "How do we live a good life?" Most of what we call Western religion, Judeo-Christian systems, are based on Plato. To appreciate Plato, we must explore the Plato-Socrates *leap of faith*. To explain, Socrates was inquiring, *"What is* virtue?", *"What is* justice?", etc., which upon inquiry was deconstructed; however, people were left in a state of confusion, disorientation, possibly even emptiness, because they realized they no longer knew what virtue was, they no longer knew what justice was. In short, they no longer had a system to operate out of. Therefore, they were left with **NOTHING**.

In *Plato's Republic*, this was a very common event. Plato reports that as Socrates was about to die, after taking the infamous hemlock, all his students were gathered around him and they were freaked out. It is this point of *freak out*, which is essential for us to look at. His students were afraid that Socrates would no longer exist. He would no longer *be*; it was an intolerable situation that he would no longer exist[11]. To resist that, two things occurred. Socrates proposes his theory and suggests that when you die, you do not die, but rather there is an invisible part of you called a soul and that soul continues. The soul concept would become the cornerstone of what would become Platonism. Plato changes the frame of Socrates' work of inquiry as not a critical inquiry; rather Plato reframes it and *leaps* to defend against death, perplexity, confusion, and the emptiness of not knowing, which occurs by "staying with" *non-existence*. Rather, Plato instead makes a story; he creates a *leap of faith*. Plato's story changes the course of inquiry from deconstruction to construction,

---

[11] As an aside, the rise of existentialism in the 1940s, 1950s and 1960s focused on existence and death. For now, however, we notice that this concept of nonexistence creates a leap of faith.

which becomes the foundation of the Christian Grand Narrative Story explanations. Plato shifts the purpose of inquiry and restates its purpose: to lead the soul to *the other world of ideal forms or ideas.*

Forms, according to Plato's discourse, exist in another world. Forms are the prototypes; all else, or what we see, are merely copies. For example forms could be absolute virtue, absolute justice, absolute perfection. When we see a tree, we are not seeing a tree, we are seeing an imitation, a copy of the original. The tree of trees, the essence and real presence of treeness, according to Plato, exists in another world, in the land of forms or ideas or pure ideas. In other words, behind our ideas or what we perceive, is the essence of the idea or thing that exists in another world. For Plato, when the soul dies, it goes to this land of forms to contemplate (as will be discussed later, the world of forms or pure ideas becomes the Christian Heaven). It is from this *idea* or *structural seed story* taking root that the discourse finds its spokesperson (Plato), and this mythology continues to the present. Later on, *"A"* will draw us to the difference between Platonism and existentialism; for now, briefly stated, Plato said that the essence of a thing precedes its existence; existentialists say that there must be existence first, before there is the concept of essence. (i.e. the **I AM**)

Back to Plato, once this "soul going to the land of forms" is imagined and taken as true, questions begin to arise. For example, how did the soul get here? Plato and, for the next 2,400 or more years, other philosophers (both religious and New Age) began the construction of a house of cards (concepts) built on sand (the concept of a soul going to the land of forms). In this way the primary structure, a soul going to the land of forms ("heaven"), never comes into question, rather, this structural story begets more and more seed stories (justifications). For example, Question: "How did the soul get here?" Answer: "The soul fell." Question: "Why?" Answer: "*Because* it got attracted to this lower imitation, the world of phenomena, hence the soul lost its direction. It *fell.*" Question: "How can my soul avoid this fall and return to the land of pure forms?" Answer: "If you spend a life in virtue, purity, contemplation, etc., give up desires; then upon death, your soul returns to the land of forms." This is the beginning of the seed story that began to grow, and when it sprouted, became a lens; a structure by which we view the world and frame the world in a particular way. This structure called *soul*, going to another world, *falling*, and *ascending* exists in many of our religions.

According to Plato in his famous "Allegory of the Cave," the real world is not in the cave. The cave is a shadowy reflection, the real is outside of the cave in the metaphor of the sun. Please note that metaphors are abstractions, linguistic representations, and, as such, they are fictions. Plato set up a religion, whereby souls are trapped in bodies in a cave, they cannot see the light. It implies more than *one substance*; but moreover, it implies that if you are good and do certain things and not do certain things, somehow you'll leave the darkness of the world and ascend into this light. This is a very seductive thing because for Plato the forms are permanent. And *most people seek not only their utopian Nirvana, but it also must be permanent.* As an aside, the doctrine of *impermanence* (no permanence) is a major tenet of Buddhism. However, Plato goes from the transient to the permanent, from the unreal to the real, misunderstanding that there is only *one substance*, and somehow imagining that there are two or more *substance*s.

Substance can be defined as that which has a propensity to exist. Since everything exists, therefore there is only one substance.

Spinoza

The Spiritual Path

According to Plato, the spiritual practice rests with the understanding that the soul must *turn away* from darkness (everything in *this* world) and focus the "inner eye" on this land of perfect forms or ideas. This leads to detaching the soul from the body, thus leading the soul upward toward its spiritual ascent.

Plato uses his *leap of faith* to resist death and opt for a soul going to Heaven (land of perfect ideas or forms). Albert Camus, the Nobel Prize winning existentialist author, says *"The leap of faith* (which is followed by many Christian philosophers), is not a leap of faith, but is the *leap of fear* distancing us from dealing with just the pure emptiness and absurdity of what life is." Moreover, Camus calls this *leap of faith a fall from grace*, because for Albert Camus, this leap of fear pulls people away from facing death and remaining lucid (aware).

Plato and Love

Plato believed in his heart that love was a motivating force. Let me say now that love, as we normally define it, loving a movie, loving food, loving a person, and so on, is a pleasurable biological, phenomenological feeling. There are sensations that are pleasant, which are associated with survival, and therefore are endeared. There are emotions like hate that are painful sensations, which ignite feelings of no survival, and they are painful precisely because they are associated with lack of survival. We all want love, we all hate hate. We all want pleasure, we all detest pain. But these are only feeling states. In other words, the judgment or evaluation of feeling states are survival based and rests, on the biological level, on the existential fear of death. Plato, however, exclaimed that there was a love much more essential in the land of the forms, hence it is something that everyone would want.

In Christianity the pleasurable feeling of love becomes associated with ascendancy and is then projected onto God. Hate, which is associated with falling, is projected onto the devil and the darkness. These structured seed stories are so pivotal, so deeply ingrained as to organize most Western cultures. I am not stating here in any way that Plato is some kind of incredible fool or genius, rather, he was the mouthpiece for a structural seed story that has both ignited and enslaved the world.

Socialized Spiritualized Love

In this way, love is pleasurable and becomes spiritualized and socialized. You are told that if you do these good things, you will experience love for all of eternity; and, if you do these bad things, you will experience eternal pain and hate for all of eternity. Love becomes spiritualized, and people naturally wish they could have this biological experience for eternity; and contrariwise, hate is unspiritual, read as a bad thing, which you get if you don't do the "right" things.

SUMMARY

Plato, Aristotle and the Platonists

Aristotle was Plato's student. Aristotle continued positing that there was a world soul, and that this world soul was somehow moved or moved forward by a *primary mover*. This primary mover, which Plato called *the good*, suggests a separate originary source point outside space-time, somewhere "out there," that moves all of this world. Later, of course, we could call this *God*.

The Ethics of Life

It is important to discuss this in terms of several definitions. For example, first, neoplatonists believe that there is an *intelligible form*, which, you could say, is something like virtue or justice. This intelligible form is a prototype and becomes a standard, a standard of judgment, a standard of behavior, a code of behavior, a way of being, doing and acting. Later, it will become some form of an ethics. Second, there is an *origin* or an order to this cosmos. It is not a random event. Third, the soul is some kind of an immortal being that is separate from the body. The soul is more like the "perfect forms" than it is like the body. The soul has fallen into this world of change and embodiment where it does not belong. The soul is kind of an intermediary state between the body and this other world. The soul is some kind of reflection in the divine eye. The soul, when it turns away from everything in contemplating the divine mind, has kind of a blessed life.

For Plato, *spiritual is defined as other-worldly*. The story of the fall of the soul into this world occurs when it descends into some kind of body, because there is some kind of bad thing, some kind of vice, that the soul got attracted to. Virtue (these good qualities) arises when the soul pulls away from the world, purifies itself somehow, and then it can see these divine forms. Later, we will see that the Christian world adapts this story of *ideal* forms to create a hierarchy of forms. These ideal forms become angels, and so we can see that these angels, and sometimes "fallen angels" like Satan, become key players in the Christian story.

Finally in Plato's story, the soul is the part of you that is divine. Now, 2,500 years later, people believe that this divine part of themselves is something they need to integrate and be a part of. This becomes a key principle in the development of what we call *Western spirituality*.

I hope this was helpful.
"R"

If you didn't know about this soul before you were born, you don't experience it now, and you won't know about it after you die— why is it so important?

David Hume

CHAPTER 4

GOD AS AN
ARCHETYPAL STRUCTURE

If we trace the history of God or gods, what we notice is that the story of God, or many gods begins as a *mythology*, a structure, an archetype. A mythology is an explanation of *why*, *what*, or *how* things occur. Noted anthropologist Claude Levi-Strauss suggests that myths are a metaphor, a way to understand and reconcile life's problems, contradictions, and paradoxes. Others, like Sir James Frazer suggest that it is a structure that attempts to organize and explain what is, and Bronislaw Malinowski and Andrew Long saw myth as used to justify rituals, roles, and society's rules. Some refer to myths as a *early indigenous science*. Others, like Carl Jung, mistakenly believe mythical images are universal, rather than cultural as they have been shown to be.

An archetypal structure, for our purposes, is an anthropomorphic representation used to explain why and how things got the way they are; their main purposes are to provide comfort, and to bring order to chaos. For example, humans anthropomophize and fabricate (project) God as having a physical human-like body. Now these anthropomorphic "human-like" Gods have choices, wants, desires, anger, sadness, fear, love, wrath, and teaches lessons. This is an anthropomorphic projection of human qualities onto a "formless being," which does not have a nervous system. This anthropomorphic explanation is a process whereby a human being with a nervous system projects itself onto something that does not have a nervous system, it could be God, a tree, a virus, etc. In short, the mythology presents God as a person. He speaks, desires, has a plan, teaches lessons, God is like a person, almost like a father or a mother, and often is even referred to as a father and a mother (in India, *Baba* means father and *Amma* or *Mata* means mother). God gets angry with you; he chooses certain people, he doesn't choose other people; he teaches lessons; he always loves; some people get rescued, and some people get punished (go to Hell); and some people get saved and some people don't. He has desires; he has feelings; and, most importantly, if you do not worship him the way you "should," you get his wrath. He is dangerous. Therefore, this God does things, just as a real person in the real world does things, this is an anthropomorphic representation.

In the story of religion, there are certain ways to behave around God, there are certain rituals, ways of reaching this archetypal structure. There are sacred places, certain techniques, certain ways called a "path" to reach God. The worship of God, as an archetypal representation whereby "I" worship this source of power "out there," which gives things or does things to me. He/she is in charge, whether it be Zeus or God, has been going on since the beginning of time.

WHERE DOES THE POWER
OF ARCHETYPES COME FROM?

The question that often emerges, how is that, if we go to a temple, or a retreat center, and we chant the name of God or we repeat the name of God, there is a certain feeling tone or atmosphere that occurs. Why? Because the nervous system has a fight-flight- freeze-*pray* survival response. In short, under extreme stress, this pray-to-God response gets triggered in the brain, and we pray. The brain via the pineal gland releases DMT (a neurotransmitter) and we feel more relaxed and comfortable. Moreover, you are evoking, focusing your attention on an archetype, an archetypal "energy." There are many archetypes of God, whether you have God or a hierarchy of gods and deities, all of this cosmology creates order, a cosmos in order, which gives us comfort, peace, order, safety, and no chaos.

Archetypal "Energy" Patterns

In *The Way of the Human, Volume III*, archetypes are discussed as condensations of the physics dimensions and forces: energy, space, mass, time, electromagnetics, sound, light, etc. The "power" of archetypes is that they are primordial structures made of the condensed physics dimensions and forces.

Here are two critical points to understand in dealing with archetypes:

1. That they have a power, but the archetype is intermittently made of the physics dimensions and forces, which are condensed **NOTHINGNESS**. Noted physicist, John Wheeler, said **"NOTHINGNESS** is the building block of the universe."

2. Spiritual paths are archetypal, discursive structures, and as such, you cannot go beyond an archetype (spiritual path) by "acting out" the archetype (spiritual path). The archetype must
be "seen" as a discursive structure and then it
must be dismantled (deconstructed). Thus, acting-out an archetypal structure we can see in
people who have "done" "spiritual practice"
for years, and yet they still suffer. Simply stated:
Performing an archetypal path by doing the rituals of the archetypes keeps you stuck in the archetype. You cannot get out of an archetype by
doing its rituals; you always get stuck. Archetypal rituals only beget more archetypal rituals.

The Myth of Creation

The explanatory myth of creation (the how and
why myths) exist in the Greek stories whereby the
myth of creation began with chaos. Chaos can be defined as out-of-order, out of control, or the **NOTH-
INGNESS** that existed before the creation of the universe. In Greek, the chaos was a *yawn*, a pause. In the
East, the space between.

In the West, creation comes from **NOTHING**, there
is only God. The myth or story of creation in each culture is different and always contains a logos, or center or source, called (fill in the blank), from which the
world springs. The source can be called God who is always in control, the creator, the first mover, the origin,
and is the source.

Countless rituals or symbolic representations of
how to reach God. In some stories of God, you make
a convenant (deal) with God, in other words, you do

these things, "spiritual practices," and God will pay you back with rewards: bliss, love, Nirvana, Heaven, a good life, enlightenment, etc.

This story is kind of a capitalistic/consumer God, whereby you trade virtue, detachment, and rituals, and she/he gives you good things in return. The trade is supposed to be fair; but if you do not get these things, then we imagine and rationalize that God will straighten it out later, or has other plans for you.

With Love
"R"

How can I become what I already am?

Friedrich Nietzsche

CONVERSATIONS WITH "A"

Philosophical Traps

CHAPTER 5

CAUSE AND EFFECT

"R": The noted 17th century philosopher, David Hume, considered by many to be the most important skeptical empiricist, speaks directly about cause and effect. First some quick definitions: An empiricist believes in experiences. A skeptical empiricist does not. At first blush, particularly in light of the human potential movement, how could anyone be told not to trust his or her experience? However this philosopher of the 1700s saw something that has been proven scientifically only in the last half of the 20th century; namely, *we never experience things directly*. Rather, all experiences are mediated through the human nervous system (sensory organs and brain). Hence, experiences are abstracted reproductions that represent less than 1% of the billions of 'bits' of information that are received, a tiny "sensory map" of a huge "territory of energies." Moreover, not only is the nervous system able to "get" or *transduce* or utilize only a tiny fraction of the information that it receives, it is also *late*, which means that actions, choices, perceptions, and volition have already occurred by the time the "I" or perceiv<u>er</u> of an action or choice has been produced by the brain and nervous system.

What David Hume is saying is that all your experiences, all your impressions, are representations. Everything that "you" experience began as a sensation, i.e., through the senses. Since everything began as a sensation and impressions are representations of sensations, then everything that you experience, along with the "I" or perceiver that is experiencing it, is an abstraction of sensation. Since everything is an abstraction of sensation and is only a nervous-system-mediated representation, no one can actually know the world as it is. It is for this reason that sensation (a "primary," earlier abstraction) would be much "closer" to what is, than a perceiver's or "I"'s conclusion or belief (a "secondary," later abstraction) about what is[12].

According to Hume, concepts consist of associations. Associations are produced in these ways: 1) By *resemblance*; in other words, "I" see this chair. This chair looks like other things that are called chairs, which you sit on. Therefore, "I" 'know' "I" can sit on it. It is not the original chair, but I make the association that it is a chair through *resemblance*. We learn to make sense of the world by noticing similarities, and we categorize people and things according to the similarities or resemblances that we notice. Once we have a "mental" category of things that resemble each other, we can create a generalization about 'all' things in that category. In daily life, the brain and nervous system use many of these generalizations for making sense of the world and guiding our attitudes and behavior in the world. We go through life telling ourselves things like this:

---

[12] Let "me" be clear without confusing the issue so early in the text: "There is no *what is*."

"All women are (fill in the blank)"; "All lawyers are (fill in the blank)"; etc. This is how we function on the basis of resemblance. 2) *Space-time*, if an Event X happened here, and at about the same time and the same location in space, Event Y preceded X, then we may think that Y, caused X. We infer, for example, that if "I" take my glasses off a table, then you leave the room, and "I" put the glasses four feet away from the table, your nervous system infers that the glasses moved from Point A (on the table) to Point B (4 feet from the table) because someone moved it. Events are *conjoined*, either because they *resemble* other events, or are fused together if they resemble other events, or if they occur in *proximity* of their event. 3) And most important is *cause and effect*. "I" look at an event and "I" assume that the event just preceding this event caused this particular event to happen. This is where it gets tricky. Everything that you see is an abstraction or representation of your nervous system. What you see is not what is. Your nervous system gives you the impression, the idea, the concept that Event B caused Event A. This view of *B causes A*, and the "I" that holds this view, is an abstraction of the nervous system. To illustrate, let's say for example, that "I" believe that the future will be like the present. Now, I have no way of knowing this, but "I" notice from "my experience" that the past resembles the present, and the present seems to resemble what will happen in a few minutes from now, in the future. The nervous system through omitting billions of stimuli, selects out only a few and produces representations in a linear fashion. For this reason, (THIS IS IMPORTANT!!!) if "my" experience tells me that cause and effect is true, then cause and effect is true. *The problem is that <u>the experience of cause and effect is also an abstracted representation</u> of what is. It is not what is.* This is extremely important. An experience is an abstracted representation, and an experience is produced by omitting billions of stimuli and selecting out only a small fraction. Therefore, <u>experiences of cause and effect are abstracted representations that cannot validate cause and effect</u>.

We must understand that cause and effect is an "experience" and all experience is a representation and abstraction. Therefore, a person's experiences and the resulting perceptions and conclusions represent less than 1% of incoming stimuli. The nervous system creates the illusion of cause and effect, according to Hume, as a custom or habit. Now, in the 21st century, we might say that the brain "evolved" to create cause and effect relationships as a survival mechanism, as a way to increase the brain's (and the person's) chance of survival.

"R"

"STRUCTURAL SEED STORY"
In most spiritual systems there is some form
of cause and effect. What about cause and effect?

"A": What you see as reality are snapshots, there is reality-space-reality-space-reality-space . . . snapshots. The illusion is that one snapshot causes the next snapshot, which causes the next snapshot, etc. In other words, there is an illusion of cause and effect. It is personal consciousness, or what is called "self-consciousness,"

which creates this illusion and links these representational pictures into a coherent whole, which prevents us from seeing the hole or gap or discontinuity between thoughts, ideas, and situations. This in-between space is called "Bardo" in Buddhism, "discontinuity" by Michel Foucault, and "dissemination" by Jacques Derrida. Nevertheless, "you" can notice the "space" between thoughts or discourses and how one discourse does not relate to another. There is even a meditation where "you" notice the lack of connection between thoughts.

For example, if you are walking down the street, "you" can notice, first, that you are thinking about work, then about a friend, then a vacation, then your love life. It is consciousness that creates the illusion of continuity and one-to-one cause and effect relationships. *There is no separate "you" that creates cause and effect; rather, the nervous system does it as the "I" arises* and is aware of it. In this way, everything just happens, then later the "I" claims responsibility or doership! *The "I" is contained within the discourse.* This is why Buddha said, "There is no separate individual self-nature." There is *no independent origination.* What you see is an appearance, but it is not an appearance *of* something (i.e., the nervous system abstracts from **NOTHING!!**).

David Hume said, "The creating of cause and effect is a habit of the mind [nervous system]." He maintained that cause and effect relationships occurred when 1) two events occur close together and get conjoined, 2) there is a resemblance between two events, or 3) they occur in space-time near one another.

The belief in cause and effect re-enforces the "I" and its illusions of "'I' caused this," "'I' do that," "'I' can cause or create something else," "'I' can create a different effect out here by presenting a different action or cause." This is a misunderstanding; one who believes this does not realize that this "I" is constantly arising, space, arising, space, arising, space, along with the idea, or discourse, which is also called a text in Postmodernism.

It is pivotal to understand that the nature of the nervous system's illusion or mirage carries with it the illusion of cause and effect and the great illusion, of Karma. Karma is the nervous system's abstracted illusion of cause and effect. There is no Karma, because there is only *that one substance*, call it Buddha-nature, call it Brahman, call it **void**, call it *the substance*, call it THAT. Consequently, an "I," in the context of a mirage, might delude itself enough to think that the "I" is the cause, or that there is an effect related to a separate individual cause, or *this* separate event caused *that*. The "I," and the perceiver of what is seen, is a representation an abstraction, which arises after the event or action has already happened.

*"The conception of cause and effect
is fundamentally erroneous, and must be
replaced by a quite different notion,
laws of change. Sequences (like A causes B)
in the traditional forms of causation have not
been found in nature. Everything in nature is
apparently in a state of continuous change,
so that what we call one event turns out
to be really a process."*

Bertrand Russell

CHAPTER 6

GOD

THE PURPOSE OF THIS SECTION IS NOT TO DESTROY GOD, BUT TO DE-CENTER A LOCALIZED CONCEPT OF GOD AS A SEPARATE DEITY, WHO FLOATS IN THE SKY OR "OUTSIDE" THE UNIVERSE.

ALL WORDS, INCLUDING THE WORD "GOD," ARE ABSTRACTIONS, BINARY, DUALISTIC, AND CARRY WITH THEM THESE LINGUISTIC PROPERTIES. ALL WORDS CARRY WITH THEM THE LINGUISTIC ILLUSION OF A SEPARATE THING, A SEPARATE LOCALIZATION, IN THIS CASE A LOCALIZED ENTITY, WHICH OCCUPIES ITS OWN SEPARATE LOCATION IN SPACE-TIME, AND WHICH HAS A SEPARATE "PERSONAL" ESSENCE OR A SEPARATE "PERSONAL" PRESENCE.

"A"

"STRUCTURAL SEED STORY"
*Could you say something about the story
that "we are chosen"?*

"A": It is imperative in most spiritual systems, as a sales pitch, that *I am chosen (You are chosen)*, that's how we got to do this spiritual path; this sells: the notion that "you" are something special. There are two problems contained within this, first it implies a choos<u>er</u>, as if there is some kind of a separate force "out there" that points its finger and says *"You're chosen."* Next it also implies a choos<u>ee</u>, an "I" who is chosen. There is only *one substance*, therefore, there cannot be a choos<u>er</u> or a choos<u>ee</u>. Hence, the statement held in the understanding of *one substance* should be discarded.

"STRUCTURAL SEED STORY"
The will of God is the cause of all things.

"A": There is no cause and effect. There is no independent separate thing that causes or brings about a particular separate individual effect. There is only *one substance*. It is like saying a water droplet (person) someplace in the ocean, could cause the ocean (world) to move. It's the entire ocean that's moving. In the same way, since there is only *one substance* and since there is only the ocean, there is no God separate from the ocean itself. All that occurs is made of *the substance*, all that doesn't occur is made of *the substance*, but you could not even say *that* because there would have to be a separate "I" to say it was so. And so, to imply very

subtly that there is a separate God who has a will and that causes things is non(sensical). If everything is the ocean, a separate, individual God, which causes droplets of the ocean to move, or teaches a water droplet a lesson so that it can realize that it is part of the ocean implies a separate God with some agenda, and a separate "I" that needs to learn some lesson. It's all one flow and *one substance*.

"R": This reminds me of David Hume's insistence that the mind (nervous system) conjoins events together to form cause-and-effect relations where none exist. What *"A"* seems to be talking about is that when things cannot be explained, to fill in this gap of uncertainty the nervous system creates a cause, in this case, a separate God, since the nervous system cannot find a cause.

"STRUCTURAL SEED STORY"
We get into Heaven not by our wits,
but by the grace of God.

"A": Let's look at all of the assumptions in this: 1) that an "I" gets something or goes somewhere; 2) there's a *place* called Heaven that has a separate location that is made of a different substance; 3) that there is a separate being or God that grants this certain thing "here" that gets us into a place which is not here, made of a different substance than here; 4) that God has this will, which somehow could be separate from "our" will. which is made of a different substance than itself.

All of these imply different substances. If there is *only one substance*, how could there be a Heaven or a

Hell, how could there be a separate God made of a different substance who has a separate individual will, or a separate self or soul.

"STRUCTURAL SEED STORY"
We come to know God by his words.

"A": The best way to know God, according to some, is to look at the Bible. These are the words of God. According to the *Siva Sutras*, "all bondage is caused by sound," in other words, *language*. It is language that forms the "I"; prior to the formation of language, you are not. In this way, the "I" along with all abstracted concepts do not exist outside of language. To illustrate, think the thought "I feel good." Now, think the thought "I feel good" without using words. Thoughts and words are dependent upon each other, you cannot have one without the other. Ludwig Wittgenstein even goes so far as to say that, all words are just names for things, and that thinking is just naming things, in this regard all systems of thought about "I" or "other" or the nature of the universe are simply a system of communication, which he calls a *language game*. Since in neuroscience it is said that thoughts and speech come after the action or event is even perceived and arises from a body, then all thoughts are body-based and dependent on a body. The "I" and perception, come after action, event, and even speech occur. The "I" and the perceiver is an abstraction, and prior to its appearance there is no "I," and *you are not. The "I" you call you is a linguistic representation, a description of what is*, although there is no "*what is.*"

Moreover, sound has no meaning without a brain. The auditory part of the brain transduces (trance-duces) the sound converting it from sound into meaning and words.

"STRUCTURAL SEED STORY"
*Everything you get is a gift,
and you should be grateful to God.*

"A": This is an old philosophy which seems to have become part of the new-age philosophy; that whatever comes to you is a gift from God, an opportunity for you to work on yourself. Opportunities are what "I" call *spiritual reframes. Reframes are defenses.* Generally speaking, things are reframed in order to resist, diminish, and deny, experiences that you don't want to have. For example, if "I" have an experience of fear, "I" can reframe that as an internal motivator. Reframing defends you against something that you don't wish to feel, whatever that may be. Many of the so-called new therapies are into reframing pain as an opportunity, believing that if you change the frame, or re-frame, you change the experience. The problem is that the reframe(ing) of anger or fear, for example, is made because it is already under the frame of "anger or fear is bad." Therefore, when you reframe you add a new frame, i.e., fear is an internal motivation on top of an earlier frame, "fear is bad." In this way, you are adding another layer onto the earlier layer. Why? Because you don't want to feel it. Although this might give temporary relief, it makes it more difficult to unpeel the onion's layers.

A spiritual re-frame is *"everything that you get is a gift."* If you are walking down the street and someone sticks a gun in your face and steals your money, I wouldn't call it a gift, I would call it a theft. Now we could re-frame it as a gift and an opportunity, which some spiritual and psychological systems do, but this only keeps the psychological *language game* going and is spiritually and psychologically inaccurate, and in the long run, detrimental. For example, *I should be grateful to God.* It implies there is somebody or something "out there" that's in charge of the entire game, that's manipulating, moving things around, so that I can get these opportunities to grow. The abstracted concept and story of growth, even spiritual growth, is an abstracted story. If there is only *one substance,* how could there be a "grow" or a "not grow," or "progress" or "not progress"? This story can be discarded.

Spiritual or unspiritual exists in language only, it is a language game that is derived from words and concepts, which arise neurologically as an organizing abstraction after actions and events have already occurred. There is no progress or growth outside of the word "progress" or "growth." Progress and growth exist in language only. The question "I" would ask is, "If there were no language, would you be?" Even if your answer is yes, it's a word called "yes." "Yes" is part of an abstracted language; without language what does "yes" mean? All you can do is go blank, this is, the nonverbal *I am.* Even the word or concept of awareness is "perceivable" and "knowable," and as such, it is a representation, which is an abstraction, which exists in language only: there is no awareness outside of the word "awareness." Even the "experience" of awareness is an "experience," and as such, it is a representation. Because awareness requires an awar<u>er</u>, experi<u>encer</u>. Nirvana means extinction; hence, just as there is no Walden, there is no thing or place that is Nirvana. This could be why the Buddha rarely spoke much about Nirvana.

"STRUCTURAL SEED STORY"
God created us in his image.

"A": God narratives are discourses, which contain a separate individual God that forms this separate individual us in his image. The discourse implies God has an image. It implies God is a person. These stories are anthropomorphic projections because they imagine that God is a person who creates things, has anger, has wrath (like a person), in fact God acts like a person in most of the Bible. God gets angry, God gets jealous, God gets annoyed, God punishes, God praises, God saves people, God loves people, God hurts the wicked, God does good things; these are all anthropomorphic, meaning that these human qualities are projected from a human nervous system onto God which has no body and no nervous system. Moreover, to say there is an "us" or a "him," implies that there are two substances. If there is only *one substance* how could it create something other than itself? If everything is the same substance, how could something be created, or how could something be destroyed? It can only shift from one perception to another perception and actually can never change, it is always the same.

Prior to Socrates, there was a debate between Parmenides and Heraclitus. Parmenides said that nothing changes or moves. Heraclitus said everything changes and moves. Both of them are correct. *"As the substance,"* nothing changes. *As something separate from the substance, a* witness, everything changes or moves. Both were correct, and since both the witness<u>er</u> and the wit-ness<u>ed</u> are the same substance, neither is true. In other words, *"as the substance"* there is no substance, because if everything is made of the same substance, there is neither, witness nor substance, neither **void** nor know-er of the **void**. This is *Sunyata* in Buddhism, and upon "realization" you understand the "answer" to the fa-mous Zen Koan, "What is the sound of one hand clap-ping?"

"STRUCTURAL SEED STORY"
*In India they say God or source created us
as a play or a game, in Sanskrit a "lila"?*

"A": The God playing a game is a Grand Narrative which contains a discourse that there's a game, and that this thing out there called "source" created all of this universe so that it could play. It (the source) pre-tended not to be what it was so it could "experience." The meta-narrative (Big Story) is an anthropomorphic explanation in order to give reasons for the world. My-thology gives an explanation, but it is a mythology, an abstracted story, a discursive structure, which is to be discarded. There is only *one substance*, and *there is no Nirvana that is.*

"STRUCTURAL SEED STORY"
There is a rational God who is present and has a presence.

"A": The narrative of presence and natural implies God has got some kind of intellect (like ours). Here we run into the same anthropomorphic situation. A God with some kind of plan, some kind of design. This is like Saint Augustine's designer narrative: the universe seems to have an order to it and, therefore, there must be a master who ordered it, or since a watch has a design to it, there must be some kind of master designer. The *one substance* is the *one substance* is the *one substance*, and the *one substance* does not have a "presence" but is everything. There is no centralized God separate from the substance or a "you" or "me." Everything is made of the same substance. Words give the illusion of a separate presence. But present or presence or existence is a linguistic abstraction only. Appreciate that *the word "illusion" means something that appears to be there, but is not there.*

This leads us to one of the most subtle deconstructions of the postmodern era; proposed by Jacques Derrida, it is the concept of presence. The concept of presence and essence was Plato's, who suggested that when we say a word like "tree," it represents a prototypical tree that exists in another world and is and has the "real" presence and essence of the tree. Ferdinand de Saussure, and later Jacques Derrida, showed that words are arbitrary, conventional and cultural, and that these words, which he called *signs*, had no original presence or prototype that was behind them. This is profound because it means for example that there is no virtue (with a capital V), outside of the word or how we use the word "virtue." Even more startling is that words or sounds are not placed upon an object like chair, or tree, or table. Rather, the word or sound does *not link a word with a thing, but a word (signifier or sound) or sign is linked with a concept of a thing, not the thing itself!!!*

"R": ("I" began to remember *"A"* saying "There is no thing itself," and that the nervous system abstracts from **NOTHING**.)

"A": We can take this even further than either Saussure or Derrida by stating that without a nervous system, there is **NOTHING**. Through the mediation of the brain and nervous system, objects that were not, appear to be. The sound or words link a sound to an object, which is a constructed abstraction that was produced by the nervous system; the words do not link to an actual object, but to a <u>constructed, abstracted object fabricated by a nervous system through abstracting</u>. This is fundamental to dismantling (deconstructing), and it is fundamental to Madhyamika (Middle Way) Buddhism and destabilizing the solidity of the object, or world. In the Diamond Sutra, Buddha says, "There is no world that is there."

Derrida takes Saussure even further by saying that what gives things their meaning is not their presence but their absence. This is very subtle because there is a word *then a gap* (absence), then another word happens. However in the gap there is a *trace* or track of the first word that remains even in the absence of a word. Going even further than Derrida is *Buddha's Heart Sutra*: Form (solidified trace) is emptiness (unsolidified trace) or subtle trace which is form, because absence is as important as presence. Presence, is an abstracted experience of an "I" and, as such, should not be confused with something that actually is; rather it is an abstraction, a word that *stands in* for the absence-presence play.

Moreover Derrida suggests that the history of philosophy is a search for the logos: a transcendental presence beyond linguistic structure, and that this logo-centered impulse is binary[13] and seeks a beyond like God, Being, or presence that answers all questions. Ultimately, in **post-deconstruction**, when this impulse (which produces a "seeker I-dentity") collapses, then *You Are NOT*.

"STRUCTURAL SEED STORY"
*There is a constant participation of God
that can and does influence the world.*

"A": This God Grand Narrative discourse contains a separate something out there, which somehow guides or constructs the universe over here. There is only *the substance*.

"STRUCTURAL SEED STORY"
God sends messengers to redeem and save man.

"A": In the messenger/redeemer/savior meta-narrative discourse, something separate from us sends a messenger, a guide through the ethos to save this creature

---

13 A set of two terms, in which one term is privileged over the other and considered better, closer to the logos (God, source) than the other; for example, being/becoming (being is closer to the logos than becoming), soul/body, emptiness/form, etc.

called "man" "woman" and offer him salvation. To be saved means to be saved from death. So, this imaginary separate substance sends messengers that come directly from him or her. This separate God who sends a separate savior to save a separate individual man or woman, is both anthropomorphic and representational at best, and early indigenous science and an abstraction at worst.

"STRUCTURAL SEED STORY"
God has a reason, an interest in you personally,
and in the world.

"A": There is no reason outside of the word *reason*!! Reason exists in language only!! Reason seeks a separate cause (logos) for occurrences. If there is only one substance, then there is no separate cause.

Moreover, it could be said that the nervous system abstracts a reason for things occurring in its attempt to organize chaos and survive better. But the "I," which imagines it has volition and performs actions, arises later, after the action has already taken place. This story of an outside source, which is actually interested in "you" personally, is both primitive and anthropomorphic, not to mention child-like in the psychological language game. *The substance* does not know you or itself, so how can *it* have an interest in you <u>personally</u>?

"R": In the psychological language game, it is like having a mom and dad out there who are interested in you personally, and interested in what happens to you. They become magical mommy and daddy who are all-knowing, all-good and all-powerful. In psychology's

language game, you are transferring magical Mommy or Daddy onto God or Guru, who now has a personal interest in your being or growth.

"STRUCTURAL SEED STORY"
You can make a covenant, a deal, or a pact with God.

"A": The covenant narrative, contains a discourse of getting paid with bliss, love, and salvation for work (spiritual practice). You do these rituals, which they call a path, and God gives you protection, liberation, and bliss. This is anthropomorphizing, spiritualizing, and it is infantile.

Most importantly, it implies, more than *one substance*, and it implies that *the substance* has an agenda or plan, which you follow to reach *the substance*. The story suggests that there is a separate external substance or source that is separate from you, which does these things, when there is only *that one substance*.

"R": In a psychological language game, we could say this is how children behave with their parents. You have a relationship with your parents, your parents say "If you do these good things, we'll give you these good things; and if you do bad things, we'll punish you." But parents give you a track, a path, a way to behave. If you behave in these ways, then you get all these good things; and if you don't, you get bad things. You're making a deal, a contract (a business arrangement), with your parents to follow their rules and play their game (path) for rewards or payments. Later, that deal is projected or transferred onto God.

"STRUCTURAL SEED STORY":
Saint Augustine believed that God is like
an architect and organizer.

"*R*": Philo, of Alexandria, interprets the creation story anthropomorphically, fantasizing that God is an architect. God is the designer with a blueprint. Even Saint Augustine later follows up with a similar theme, his story that God had a logical plan. Not to worry about death, the soul will go on.

Augustine presents his story that the world is a school whereby we reform students or souls so they can learn lessons and return to God. Augustine, like Plato, focuses on turning inward and upward to see God, and that's how you get happiness. The concept of the church (which also gets used in the form of an ashram), begins with a community of souls, united in their quest to turn inward to seek God. In this story, the probability of receiving God is determined by your "morality," your "virtues," how "purified" you are; hence, the rules or the laws become the story as to how the *language game* is played. In this way, all religions have rules (rituals) of the game, which is called your spiritual practice or your spiritual path, practiced in a community of souls, which is a church, ashram or school. The souls keep getting purified so they can go back to their original place, somewhere in Heaven, and in the end, get a unification with God.

Augustine's God discourse that God has a plan and an order for you, or that there is an order, and you have a place, provides a defensive myth for existential pain. How can all this be so if there is only *one substance* with no qualities, no attributes, no frames of reference and no references to frame?

"STRUCTURAL SEED STORY"
God brings you out of darkness into light.

"A": The dark-light mythologies get turned into a God narrative of darkness and light. There is even a famous anthropologist, Max Müller, who believes that mythologies were allegorical, like darkness (night) being chased away by light (the sun); in other words, battles between darkness and light. Here, not only do we now have a separate individual substance called God out there and a separate individual, "you," we also have two other substances. We have a "good" substance called light and a "bad" substance called dark, and a separate individual God who brings a separate individual "you" from a separate individual bad substance called *darkness* into a separate individual good substance called *light*. If there is only *one substance*, then how could any of these possibly exist?

"STRUCTURAL SEED STORY"
The path says, focus on God. Do not rebel or resist.
Have a relationship with God.

"A": In path narrative stories, a way out of pain is provided. Here it is: An "I" with a relationship to God. This implies an "I" that it is separate from God and an "I" that must develop a relationship to it. Why is it that the onus for relationship is always on "you" and not on God? Hold on to the understanding, *"there is only one substance."* Once you start bringing in God and God's Will, then we are automatically into separate substances, and somehow a "you" that can fail in your spirituality.

"STRUCTURAL SEED STORY"
God wounds in order to purify and heal.

"A": This is worse than a God explanation narrative, it is a classic spiritual reframe and denial, which later progressed into God giving lessons, and opportunities for growth. *Reframing is a defense*, you change the frame of reference or *language game* to make it sound more positive rather than negative "as if" there is a thing called negative and positive, rather than only *one substance.* Don't fall for this incredible story, that there is a separate substance, a centralized God, who is working on you all the time, and that he hurts you in order to purify and heal you!! Why would a centralized God have to hurt you? If a centralized, localized God was all powerful, all knowing, all good, then if he wanted you to learn these things, why would he have to hurt you or wound you to do it? Now, should the answer be, "'You' won't look otherwise"? But if God is all-powerful, then God could get you to look without kicking the shit out of you. Reframing creates more and more reframing. All of it is a story; and if they are not taken apart, you will be constantly reframing yourself into greater and greater pain and putting new linguistic layers on top of existential pain.

"STRUCTURAL SEED STORY"
God crushes pride, which gives you the Grace of God.

"A": If we have a centralized, localized God that is all knowing, all powerful, all loving, and all good, then why would he/she at first give us pride. Because if, in the beginning, there was only God, the Word was of

God, everything was God; then nothing was separate from God. If we say that nothing is separate from God, then why would God create things that would have pride, which he has to crush? If there is only God in the beginning, and there is only God now. There was only *one substance* in the beginning; there is only *one substance* now. Therefore, what is doing the crushing or not crushing. Moreover, if the "I" is an abstraction that arises after the action has taken place, how could we blame an "I" for pride if the prideful behavior occurred before the "I" person was even there? There is no "I," no blame, and no praise for an "I"'s pride that arises after the "I" even came into existence. There is *only one substance.* Some say God gave man/woman free will. This is a great argument for self-blame; but only a sadistic God, who was supposed to be omnipotent, would give a wo/man free will, knowing that he/she could hurt themselves, not a "loving God."

In India they say, "Man is much smarter than God, he knows all about good and bad, high and low, sin and virtue. God doesn't know anything about that. God just *is*."

*A Separate, Centralized, Localized Individual
God Exists in Language Only*

**There is No Separate, Centralized, Local-
ized Individual God Outside of the Abstracted
Word "God"**

"A"

"STRUCTURAL SEED STORY"
God creates everything perfectly.

"A": *The substance is the substance is the substance.* We have to let go of this localized, separate, centralized God story (grand narrative) that *He* is perfect and we screw up or are sinners. If there is only *one substance* and God is *THAT one substance*, then God is as big, or even bigger, a screwup as we are because he/she is an omnipotent all-powerful being who lets us do these things.

There is no *God separate from "us" outside of the word "God, which implies a separate God." God (which implies a separate entity) exists as an abstraction in language only.* There is no "perfect" or "not perfect." Things occur or don't occur, just like waves in the ocean happen or they don't happen. It is *the substance,* whatever arises comes from *the substance.* Whatever subsides goes back to *the substance,* but it is all still *the substance.*

"STRUCTURAL SEED STORY":
There is a guiding reason, a guiding light, or God.

"A": This story suggests that there is some kind of very high reason (with a capital *R*) out there, and a God which is separate, which has such a reason and a purpose and a guiding light. Reasons come from the neurotransmitters (chemicals coming together in the brain) and arises after the action and event and perception and "I" as an abstraction created by the nervous system *after* experiences and actions already have occurred. The concept of light is "prior" to the "I" level,

but the concept of light is "after" **THE NOTHING-NESS (THE SUBSTANCE)**[14]. The **NOTHINGNESS** or that substance is "prior" to light. Light is a condensation of the **NOTHINGNESS,** as is sound. So, to say there is a guiding light, it is as if light were God or a something that will guide you. The thing to "understand" is that there is only *one substance.* Everything else is not. The concept of reason is an abstraction, which exists in language only. There is no reason outside of the word *reason.*

---

[14] *"R"*: See *The Way of the Human, Volume III;* Chapter: The Collective Unconscious.

The nervous system and brain
produce abstracted and fabricated reasons.

There is
No Reason
(with a capital R)
Outside of
the Word
"Reason"
and how the word
reason is used.

"A"

"STRUCTURAL SEED STORY"
God speaks, acts and does things, i.e., he redeems,
he forgives, he thinks, he has wrath, gives grace,
has rules, redeems, rescues, etc.

"A": This is the ultimate anthropomorphic exercise. We have a God separate from *the one substance*, and as a projection of the nervous system, we now have a God who acts like a person. God gets angry, God gets jealous, God has rules. God redeems. If you are good he gives grace, and if you are bad he punishes. He rescues.

"R": In a psychological *language game*, parents are God to a child.

"STRUCTURAL SEED STORY"
If you are healed of sins, you can see God.

"A": This is a classic *healing of sins* narrative that survives in every form of religion from the Yoga story, to the Buddhist story, to Christianity. The story "they" tell "you," and then "you" tell "yourself," is that "'I' am a sinner. 'I' have fallen in some way." There is no such thing as sin or falling. In this story, "'I' am a sinner," and/or "'I' have fallen"; and if "I" can be healed of all of these sins, give them up, stop them, then "I" will be redeemed in some way, and then I will see God.

"R": In a psychological language game, if I am a good boy, then I will get to see God (Mom and Dad) and if I am a bad boy, then I won't get to see God (Mom and

Dad). This psychological langauge game would require an age-regression. Good boys and girls get good things. Bad girls and boys get bad things. When a little kid gets punished and sent to his room, he will not see Mom and Dad anymore. So he says "But I'll be good"; then he will see Mom and Dad. In the psychological *language game*, it is in the process of spiritualization where you make your parents not merely magical, but you make them into gods and goddesses. When children get punished, they feel like they will never see God (Mom and Dad) again. After the punishment, when they are sorry and confess, they get to see God (Mom and Dad). They are healed. They agree not to be bad any longer, then they are absolved.

There is No
Sin, Fall, or Ascent
that Exists Outside of Language.

Sin, Fall, and Ascent
are Abstracted Words, and
When Used in a Certain Way,
They Constitute a Language Game.

"A"

"STRUCTURAL SEED STORY"
God is in Heaven above the world.

"A": In this story we have a Heaven, which is a good place where good guys go. We have Hell where bad guys go. We have a separate God. We have separate substances, all of which are not.

"STRUCTURAL SEED STORY"
God is the source.

"A": We could say *the substance* is what everything is made of. The word *Source* can be misleading because it implies that it has location, a will, and that it emanates from a center with or for particular reasons. The word *Source* carries many implications. We could say that everything is made of *the same substance*, and we can say that *the substance* is the substratum of all conceivables and perceivables rather than the Source, especially if we say God is the Source. Using the word *source* in a *language game* tends to produce many anthropomorphic inferences that are unnecessary.

There is No Origin or
Originary Source that Exists
Outside of the Abstracted Words
"Origin," "Originary,"
or "Source" and How
They are Used.

"A"

"STRUCTURAL SEED STORY"
Through Grace you can see and understand God.

"A": If you're lucky, "you" will see and understand *the substance*. If "you" are unlucky, "you" will not, and there is nothing an "I" (which arises neurologically after the event and action has occurred) can do about it. This brings us to one of the most important understandings of yoga: *YOU ARE NOT THE DOER.* One way this can be translated is that the "I" arises after the action has occurred, and then the "I" takes the blame or praise for an action, which occurred before it (the "I") even arose. This is the great illusion of doership.

"STRUCTURAL SEED STORY"
In God's world, all is always for the best.

"A": In this God narrative, we see the delusional discourse of *best*. There is no such thing as best or not best. The world is made of the *one substance*, with no best or worst. There is no good or bad, right or wrong, high or low, sin or virtue, best or not best. Things don't happen for the best. Things happen as they happen; then an abstracted "I" arises after the fact, fabricates an explanation, and declares doership.

This abstracted "I" reframes pain, as a lesson, an opportunity from God; or if it is pleasure, as a gift or a synchronicity. Someone dies, "It was for the best." The reframe is a way of resisting, denying, diminishing, or defending against pain.

The question is, without using your thoughts, memory, emotions, associations, perceptions, attentions, or intentions, what is a frame of reference? *Deframe not reframe*: The non-verbal I AM is *no frames of reference and no references to frame.*

"STRUCTURAL SEED STORY"
God allows evil so he can promote a greater good.

"A": In good-evil narrative stories the discourse centers on God. The word "God," as this outside centralized and localized force, promotes or allows bad things to happen so we can promote a greater good. Besides being a rationalization, it implies three substances: God, evil, and good, all of which are not because there is only *one substance*. Moreover, if God is all powerful, all good, all knowing, where did evil come from, and what would cause God to allow or promote that which "he" already is?

"STRUCTURAL SEED STORY"
God uses evil to give us lessons and bring us closer to him.

"A": This narrative reframe is for anthropologist Claude Levi-Strauss's understanding as to why myths were fabricated: to *mediate contradictions within a society or religion.* This is mythology, with more than one substance, an individual God, evil, you and a soul, a story of falling reframed to a story of learning, so that we can be closer to him. How can we be closer to him when we are *that one substance*? A non-centralized or non-localized God is *that one substance*. We couldn't be closer than that, *WE ARE THAT; YOU ARE THAT.*

"STRUCTURAL SEED STORY"
God tests your faith in him through pain.

"A": This sadistic God story is yet another spiritualized defensive strategy called reframing. God, some separate centralized, localized, "individual" that has a separate location and originates from a source point (a point of separate origination), has an agenda, tests us as if we are children or students taking a final examination, as if God tests your faith in him by causing you pain.

This contains the illusion that God *tests* you to see if you are worthy, to see if you are good, and to see if you really love him. This illusion can help to reframe and justify the pain of life.

Ego Yoga

The testing story, along with the concept of achievement or spiritual success could be called Ego-Yoga. In other words, are you doing your Yoga, your Bhakti Yoga, Karma Yoga, and worshiping God so you can get love, bliss, etc? Are you doing it for goodies, or are you doing it to do it. The later is selfless service, the former is *Ego-Yoga*. This testing, achievement, and attainment concept involves imagining that there is a separate, independent "I" that is doing the practice and that somehow, through doing this particular practice, this "I" will have the "experience" of enlightenment; second, that there is an experience of enlightenment, which naturally implies an experien<u>cer</u> of enlightenment (to be discussed later).

"R": This reminds me of a story of a friend of mine who was with a guru. In this guru story, people said

that if the guru touches you or hits you or smacks you, then you go into Samadhi. This one particular guru punched my friend in the face, someone asked him, "Well, did you go into Samadhi?" He said, "No it hurt, if he is such a great guru, why does he have to hurt me to put me into Samadhi? Why can't he hug me to put me into Samadhi?" In this way, the whole spiritual reframe that pain yields pleasure, or "no gain without pain," is a defensive reframe.

"STRUCTURAL SEED STORY"
Since even extreme pain is God's will, we should will it,
make God's will your will, thy will be done.

"A": Just as there is no such thing as a separate God, there is no such thing as a separate, individual will because it would require a separate individual self or soul, which, even Buddha said, is not. Buddha said, "There is no independent arising, there is no separate, individual originating." There is no separate central-ized, localized God that has a will, that wills pain or wills pleasure, gives credits and debits, and gives good things if you're good and bad things if you're bad.

"R": These are all in the psychological *language game* called age regression, whereby Mommy and Daddy, who children imagine are like a god and goddess, give you good things for good behavior and bad things for bad behavior. If you *will* what they want, and want what they *will*, then you fuse with them, which chil-dren do, and then they get the goodies. You are told that if you do this, you'll have all of the good benefits.

You're taught to *will* and want what your parents *will* and want, and then they *will love you.*

"STRUCTURAL SEED STORY"
The love of God is a hard love. It demands total self-surrender and disdain of human personality.

"A": A tough God is in these God narratives: *hard love* as opposed to soft love. It demands self-surrender. How can an individual who is not, because there's only *one substance*, surrender? How can an "I," which arises after actions and events happen, take credit (doership) for surrendering or not surrendering? This "I," which claims doership or agency for actions and events, which it had nothing to do with, is a total spiritual ego.

This disdain for human personality, suggests a person who chose, and has, a personality. The personality happened and the "I" takes the blame or praise for creating the personality along with it's actions and events, even though it had nothing to do with them. Moreover, in this story, the personality is made of a different substance. But it's all the *one substance*, so it's not a matter of hard love or soft love, good love or bad love; it's all the same substance. We must get away from this thought of an "I" making a better, more spiritual ego, i.e., nicer, more compassionate, humble, more surrendered; or less spiritual ego, i.e., angry, fearful personality. It is a never-ending process by an "I" that takes the blame or praise for what it did not do. An "I" taking the blame or praise for what it did not do (because the "I" is an abstracted representation that arises after the event or action has occurred) is the ultimate ego.

*"WHEN SOMETHING DOES NOT FIT
INTO THE "I"'S REPRESENTATION
OF THE WORLD OF SO-CALLED EXPE-
RIENCE, THE "I" CREATES ANOTHER
WORLD, OR REALM, OR DIMENSION, OR
FRAME OF REFERENCE TO HOUSE, HAN-
DLE, AND/OR TO EXPLAIN IT."*

"A"

"STRUCTURAL SEED STORY"
What about God?

"A": God, according to some, is centralized and exists outside of us in a "local" or separate location. God, according to some neurobiologists, is actually hardwired into the nervous system as a survival mechanism. When things get bad, people start praying to God. But when they really dissect what it is, they find that God is a word. All words are representations or abstractions of **NOTHINGNESS**. Since God is a word, and all words are binary and dualistic, naturally, the word *God* carried with it these linguistic properties. There is no separate centralized God outside of the word *God*. The concept of *God* arises after the concept of *I am*. Would there be an archetypal concept of *God* if there was no *I am*? If there was no *I am*, you would have no knowingness of the concept called *God*. A cat does not know about God. Only those people with a cortex can have the concept called *God*.

Fight, flight, freeze, pray, all of these are neurological survival reactions when you are under stress and things are terrible. God is a word. A word is not the thing. Therefore, God exists on the level of words, but prior to the words, is **NOTHING**. Whether words or language games called spiritual locate God "up there" or "inside," we are still locating him somewhere, which is a logocentric language game which depends on words.

CHAPTER 7

SOUL

"STRUCTURAL SEED STORY"
There is a body that is separate from a soul.

"A": The story of a soul, which exists separate from a body, and is closer to God, became famous in the West through Plato; and certainly, in some form, it is a central part of Hinduism. Plato suggested that the soul is evolving to return to God, which he called *"the good,"* its source.

Historically, in Asia, what is the difference between Hinduism and Buddhism? *Sakyamuni* Buddha was a Hindu. Buddhism was formed when he had his "realization" underneath the Bodhi tree about 2,500 years ago: *"There was no separate individual soul or self that incarnates (transmigrates) from lifetime to lifetime."* In the West, Socrates-Plato came up with this concept of a soul. Everything we experience here is a copy; and the soul, after it dies, goes back to another plane of existence that is somehow more true than this plane (This is not too dissimilar to Hinduism).

The question is, if there is *only one substance*, how can there be a separate individual soul? How can the soul be separate from the body? If there is *only one substance*, how can there be a body separate from a soul separate from a substance? They already are the *one substance.*

In the last 25 to 30 years, there have been workshops that integrate mind, body, spirit. How can you integrate what already is? The mind, the body, and the spirit already are one, and made of the same substance. Some propose that the soul is invisible and is not a part of the body, and it goes somewhere after the body dies. They explicitly say, "You can't see the soul; trust, have faith." It is *blind faith* to believe that there's a soul and that if you are *good,* then your soul goes to Heaven (the land of perfect ideas). If there is only *one substance,* how could a separate soul go to another separate place, and how could the soul be separate from the body since there is only *one substance?*

Why is the soul invisible? It's invisible because there's no such thing. The soul narrative was manufactured because people do not want to deal with the concept of death and nonexistence.

"STRUCTURAL SEED STORY"
The soul must turn away from darkness, the worldly, and focus on the light of the "other world."

"A": This story has a separate soul, a darkness as opposed to light, and worldly things that are bad. This story focuses on the "light" of the "other world."

There is only *one substance* and the realization that there is only *one substance* in a constant ebb and flow is the understanding; to "realize" *that one substance* ultimately leads to <u>*you are not.*</u>

"STRUCTURAL SEED STORY"
The soul existed before it came into the body.

"A": This is a story of a fall: A soul somehow fell from its lofty position into a body; this soul existed before, and it will exist after. This brings in three substances: the concept of soul, the concept of body, and the concept of a fall; and the story to explain the three, along with the story of time. If there is only one substance, then all three are imaginary. And, as for time, it is an abstraction that exists in language only.

"STRUCTURAL SEED STORY"
The soul doesn't belong here. It has fallen. It got attracted to bodies out of ignorance, curiosity, desire, and power.

"A": This soul story must come up with reasons and justifications that explain how and why it got here. The soul story's reason: the soul has fallen. It implies that it has fallen. It got attracted to other bodies because of problems, and all of this is based on Plato's soul concept or a Hindu concept, which Buddha said was untrue, *there is no separate individual soul or self that incarnates from lifetime to lifetime.*

"STRUCTURAL SEED STORY"
There is a self or soul that is connected to the divine.

"A": Everything is made of *the substance*, call it the divine. Every thought is *the substance*. We may call

this substance the divine substance, as the 10th Century poet, Saint Jnaneshwar did. Everything is *the substance.*

"STRUCTURAL SEED STORY"
The soul is separate and a purer form of you than the body.

"A": This discourse contends that inside of you is this purer form of you. The soul is invisible. This is like the fairy tale of "The Emperor's New Clothes." Religion is selling a story of a soul that is invisible. Friedrich Nietzsche called this the *herd mentality*; everybody goes along with it, and like the Emperor's new clothes, one day we have a child that laughs and says, "The king is naked." In the same way, the soul story was conceived and sold and everyone bought into it, but it is not true.

"STRUCTURAL SEED STORY"
There is a transmigration of souls.

"A": What differentiates Hinduism from Buddhism is that Hindus believe in a separate individual soul that incarnates again and again. Buddha "realized" that there was no separate individual self or soul, which incarnated again and again and again. Tibetan Buddhism, which is partly Hindu and partly Buddhist in this area, also somewhat follows the incarnation story.

In Advaita-Vedanta there is no reincarnation because there is no separate individual soul. In Advaita there is *one substance.* In Buddhism there is the **EMPTINESS,** and in Northern Kashmiri Tantra the substance or **EMPTINESS** is called consciousness; however **UN-DIFFERENTIATED CONSCIOUSNESS** is clearer because of all the connotations in the word "consciousness." These are all words for exactly the same thing. By understanding this, you can understand that there is no separate individual soul or self with an independent self nature with independent origination that incarnates or transmigrates from body to body.

"STRUCTURAL SEED STORY"
After death, if the soul is purified of bodily desires,
it goes to the realm of perfect prototypes or forms.

"A": This is Plato's mythological story (again, not too dissimilar to Hindu or Christian beliefs), which, like all mythology, is early indigenous science and serves as a way to explain life's contradictions and pains, and how to overcome them. The problem with mythological solutions is that the solutions are based on mythological stories used to explain life. There is only *one substance* and everything is made of the same substance, including the "I." If there is only *one substance*, then there cannot be a separate individual soul, there cannot be separate perfect essences or forms from which this world is made. It is like imagining that there is a *separate*, centralized, localized God, an invisible "something," who is *separate*, who has a blueprint and makes copies called this world from some idea or prototype. There is only *one substance*, and what the "I" perceives is the abstracted or condensed substance, which is **NOTHINGNESS**.

"STRUCTURAL SEED STORY"
Soul and body are returned, saved from death,
and resurrected

"A": This is a Christian story whereby in the past, before Jesus, they said the soul would go to another place. After Jesus, his students came up with a *new and improved religion*. Not only would the soul continue to go on, but the body lives immortally. This is the meaning of the concept of The Resurrection. Christ is put in the grave and the body arises or is resurrected from the grave. This leads his students to decide, "Well, when you die, not only is your soul saved, your entire body goes to Heaven" (if you're lucky). It is interesting because not only are religions born to resist the concept of death, but before this we had souls, and the concept of a soul went on, but that wasn't good enough. Now we have the whole body going along and going on for life everlasting and it lives on forever in the Land of Milk and Honey.

For Christians, the ultimate answer is to be saved from death; hence, the body does not die, the body gets *resurrected*. If you fear death, then this is the ticket; not only does the soul goes to Heaven, "way up there," the body goes with you; this is the meaning of the resurrection, *you never die*. You are saved from the biggest fear of all, the biggest existential crisis, the biggest concern: death and nonexistence. You are saved from that, not only on the level of soul, which none of us can see (of course, it's invisible), but your entire body will be resurrected.

What is significant about this life everlasting through faith in Christ? We are reminded of a story by

Lenny Bruce, the famous American comedian, who said, "You know that if Christ was executed now [1965], he would not have died and been crucified, he would have been electrocuted in an electric chair, and therefore, everybody all over the world, rather than wearing a crucifix, would be wearing an electric chair." The story of God is a way of handling death. As the story goes, to be saved from death and having life everlasting, even with your physical body, even if your actions are "bad," you will be saved if you have faith and believe in Jesus. The story continues. If you simply believe in resurrected Christ, you share in life everlasting. So, again if "I" give myself over to this belief structure, then when this body dies, it will be resurrected, it will live everlastingly with Jesus. Jesus will give us life everlasting. That's what it means to be saved. This is resistance to the concept of death.

Soul and Body are Made of The Substance
"*R*": Nisargadatta Maharaj said to "me":
"There is no birth.
There is no death.
There is no person.
It's all a concept.
It's all an illusion.
Now you know the nothing,
And so now you can leave."

Please note that an illusion can be defined as; *that which appears to be, but it is not.* This is why Nisargadatta's statement, "You are the child of a barren woman" is one of my favorites.

"STRUCTURAL SEED STORY"
The soul has a spark that is always with God.

"A": "I" would rather say that there is only one soul or *one substance.* There is no way you can't be with God because you already are *the substance.* If you call the substance *God,* then you already are with God, and you are made of the same substance as God. But this is not a centralized, localized God who lives somewhere like a person; it is a de-centralized, non-local God, which is *the substance.*

"R": I was once with Baba Prakashananda, and someone said, "I'm going back home to Australia, and I will miss you." Prakashananda replied, "My soul, your soul, same soul." This could be translated as "my" substance, "your" substance, same substance. There is only *one substance.*

CHAPTER 8

NOT PLATO AGAIN

"STRUCTURAL SEED STORY"
This world is less important than the "other world."

"A": This Platonic narrative was co-opted to produce the Christian narrative, which held that these beliefs in another world were ideal forms, which later became angels that live in Heaven. This world isn't true or real and the "other" world isn't true or real.

There is no true with a capital *T*; there is no real with a capital *R*. There is only *one substance*. Real and true, or a state of real or true, are linguistic representations and they exist in an abstracted language only, and are not.

"STRUCTURAL SEED STORY"
Plato suggests that what we see is a copy,
an imitation of what is, not what is.

"A": This tiny aspect of the Plato narrative is correct because the nervous system produces a representation, an abstraction. He made the mistake of concluding that if all is an imitation and copy, *then* there *must be* an original prototype of *what is* "somewhere." To

explain, "I" look at a coffee mug. "I" see a copy of the coffee mug in my head. This coffee mug in my head is a copy of another coffee mug, which is a reproduction of other coffee mugs. Even if we went back in time to see a cave man, still we have a shell that he drinks out of. If we go even farther back in time, we see a cave man who has no shell, so he drinks out of his hands. But there is no original coffee mug. Why? First of all, the nervous system abstracts from **NOTHING** a coffee mug, which is not there. Secondly, there can be no original, or origin, because the word "origin" is an abstraction that exists in language only; hence, it is not a thing in itself. Moreover, what is seen is an abstraction of **NOTHINGNESS**.

The representation you see is not the representation *of something* or *of a thing* that *is*. The representation you see is based on a perceiv*er*, which is also an abstraction of **NOTHINGNESS** and IS NOT.

Don't be confused, what is seen is not an abstraction or representation *of* something or of what is. This is destabilizing the object (in Madhyamika Buddhism [Middle Way]) as a permanent, separate entity in space-time. In Middle Way Buddhism, the "understanding" by Nagarjuna of *dependent arising*, nothing is independent, helps to destabilize the illusion of boundaries that produce the "experience" of a separate, individual self.

There is no what is. There is no Walden!!!

CHAPTER 9

DOWN WITH DESCARTES
(The Cogito)

Up With the Natural Play of One Susbstance—
One Nature

"STRUCTURAL SEED STORY"
"I think, therefore I am."

"A": *The cogito*, "I think, therefore I am." is Descartes' famous statement. Descartes, in order to deduce who he is, negates everything until he is left with only thought as proof of his existence. Since he can say, "I think," he then draws an erroneous conclusion: "therefore I am," rather than realizing that the "I am" is a thought. Descartes mistakenly concludes that because there is a thought called *I am*, which he then takes for real, and concludes I AM.

The "I am" arises biochemically, as fluids come together in the brain. The *I am* is an abstraction produced by the nervous system.

It is an interesting conclusion, but it is an inaccurate one because "'I' am the think<u>er</u>" assumes that the "<u>I</u>" thinks. More accurately, *the thinker arises with the thought itself*; the mistake is the assumption and jump or leap that the "I" thinks, and a thought which arises is what this "I" thinks. The "I" is thought and a representation that imagines it thinks. The "I" does not think; the "I" arises with the thought and the "I" mistakenly imagines that the thought belongs to it.

"STRUCTURAL SEED STORY"
The mind moves the body.

"*A*": There is no mind; the mind is a metaphor, an abstraction that describes a certain space or thing, which controls the movements of the body, and is somehow separate from the body. This rather misleading representation and metaphor of a "mind" is produced by the nervous system and it implies that if "I" can change "my" mind (which is an abstraction and representation created by the nervous system), "I" can change my body.

The concept of the mind is an idea, a metaphor, a fiction, which arises from the body. What we call the mind, i.e., thoughts, feelings, emotions, associations, perceptions, all of this arises from the body and the nervous system. Therefore, the body produces a concept called *the mind*. The mind doesn't move or produce the body. Moreover, *there is no mind*. The metaphor of the mind is a description of some mysterious substance that contains thoughts, etc. The mind is a metaphor, an abstracted fiction. The concept is yet another abstraction by the nervous system. The mind, be it the unconscious mind or the conscious mind, or just the mind, exists as an abstraction, a linguistic metaphor only.

There is no mind outside of the word *mind*. To illustrate this, when Ramana Maharishi was told by a disciple, "I have a problem with my mind," he answered, "Show me your mind."

Ludwig Wittgenstein said, "It is misleading to talk of thinking as a mental actuality. We may say that thinking is essentially operating with signs (words). This activity is performed by the hand when we think by writing; by the mouth and larynx when we think by speaking; and if we think by imagining signs (words) or pictures, I can give you no agent that thinks, I would only draw your attention to the fact that you are living a metaphor and here the metaphor is the mind as an agent." (Wittgenstein, *The Blue and Brown Books*, p. 6) All language is metaphor. All philosophy is metaphor. All writing is fiction.

"All philosophy is white mythology."

Jacques Derrida

"STRUCTURAL SEED STORY"
Why do people take on belief systems when they deny bodily function?

"A": The adoration of hermetics (belief systems) is a fusion between denying bodily functions, through socialization (which yields a dissociation), and a religious reward for repression. In other words, the reason we begin to admire a hermetic or a belief system or a model occurs because we fuse together the denial of a

bodily function (including emotions and sensations), which is part of socialization, which later often yields religious socialization. When that occurs, there is a dissociation from the body and a reward for the repression comes up with a justified philosophy. In short, it can be said that repression is painful, and to overcome the pain (which seems evil) is to try to eliminate the perceived origin of the pain, which is misperceived as desire. This leads to the search for a *repressive transcendence defense* leading to the search for an origin (God), transcendental ego, or source. Societal regulation becomes internalized and then spiritualized as "Gods laws," and desire as bad (metaphorically the devil). In this way, the internalized rules docilitize the individual.

As Spinoza suggests, everything is made of the one substance. Nature is part of the one substance.

"STRUCTURAL SEED STORY"
What is life?

"A": Two things need to be discussed here. The first is that the body, which yields the metaphor called *MIND*, is made of chemicals. The body is primarily composed of five chemical elements: carbon, hydrogen, oxygen (probably more than 95%), and small percentages of nitrogen and potassium. Everything in our bodies is made from those particular elements. Now, the question emerges, "What is life?" If you reduce everything down to chemicals, then there would be no such thing as a big difference on a chemical level between different animals and plants, which means that a concept of

living or not living is not what is actually happening. It is molecular structures in movement or in motion, combining here and decomposing there, which we call life and death. The question then is what, if anything, is the purpose or what is called self-consciousness? On a biological level, according to biologist Richard Dawkins, "Consciousness evolved to mediate the best way to get from the present state that you're in to the desired state or object that you want to have or get. Consciousness actually evolved . . . The genes actually evolved the concept of consciousness because as the world got more and more complex, it needed a decision-making apparatus as to the most efficient way to alleviate the stress or tension that one was experiencing and several options were given to obtain the desired object, resources, food, sex, or whatever." We could say, "The evolution of the capacity to simulate seems to have culminated in subjective consciousness."

From this particular biological point of view, genes have evolved consciousness and given the consciousness the ability, for example, to internally speak to itself (self-talk), to project into the future and look at potential outcomes, or to simulate a future of "what ifs" so that the evolution of this self-consciousness would be for the machinery or the body to survive better. Dawkins continues, "Perhaps consciousness arises when the brain simulation of the world becomes so complete that it must include a model of itself." In other words, what is a self? A self arises, but a self is genetically being evolved, consciousness and a conscious self, for survival reasons. Once the *simulation* is complete, you have a concept of a self operating, made of consciousness, but it has evolved from organic material, i.e., the body, the genes, and proteins. "Whatever the philosophical problem raised by consciousness, for the purpose of this story it can be thought of as the culmination of an evolutionary trend of the genes." (Dawkins, *The Selfish Genes*, p. 59)

"STRUCTURAL SEED STORY"
The mind is separate from the body, and more rational than the body, emotions, and desires. And the mind causes external physical events.

"A": The ethics of Spinoza can best override the unfortunate influence of Descartes on the Western world. To approach a natural psychology, it is imperative to look at emotional states because over the last several thousand years, both East and West have deemed some emotional states good and some emotional states bad; something to have, or something to have gotten rid of. Love, bliss, and forgiveness are good. Hatred, anger, fear, and sadness are bad. The field of psychology, as well as spirituality, has adopted this very strange position; hence, it has tried to change what is deemed bad, i.e., sadness, fear, or anger. Unfortunately both spiritual and psychological, as well as moral or ethical, philosophy have tried to transform or heal these now designated "bad" emotions in some way, which somehow implies that man or woman is outside of nature, not part of nature. If we accept that humans are part of nature, then how could nature be flawed?

We must begin by understanding two things: First, all states are binary. When we say binary we could call them polarities; for example, good/bad, high/low, right/wrong, virtue/sin, just to name a few. In this binary system, one term is considered more privileged and higher, purer, or closer to God who is designated as the origin of all things. The second term in the polarity or binary is somehow "bad," fallen, decayed, or, in short, farther away from God as the origin of all things. This *binary seed of consciousness* represents the understructure of philosophy, religion, and psychology; hence, our institutions and economics. For example, for Ronald Reagan, capitalism is closer to God, communism is the Evil Empire.

The important thing to consider is that; contained within good is bad; they move back and forth in a constant change or play. Jacques Derrida calls this a "free play." If we attempt to *freeze* either one, this leads to pain. Secondly, there is *only one substance and nature is part of that one substance*. Therefore, since *there is only one substance and nature is part of that substance*, then how could something be flawed or closer to the substance? It's for this reason that both religion and psychology (psychology being the practical arm of philosophy), have created the illusions of good emotions and bad emotions. This would be like saying that if someone were to fall down, cut his leg, and blood came out, that that would be bad. If he fell down, cut his leg, and blood didn't come out, that would be good. Everything is part of nature and everything as a part of nature has a natural response and reaction regarding emotions or feeling states. These Spinoza called *affects*. Philosophy, according to Thomas Aquinas, was the handmaiden of theology and religion. Psychology now has become the practical arm of philosophy. Hence, for philosophy, religion, and psychology, unfortunately certain emo-

tions or feelings are good and certain emotions or feelings are "bad," rather than *everything is a part of nature.*

Modern philosophers believed Rene Descartes because they believed that the mind and the body were
split into two different parts. In Descartes' story, you
had an intellectual life and a physical life. What Descartes believed and proposed (which was believed by
most of the world), is that somehow the mind chooses
the body's actions. For example, he would use the il-
lustration of the mind choosing that "I" should raise
my hand, and then the hand moves; the mind chooses
that "I" should stand up, and then "I" stand up. *This is
not true!!* This is an illusion of the nervous system. The
illusion of the nervous system is that the mind (or the
"I") chooses something and then it follows. What actually happens is that the nervous system does it before
the "I" and perceiv*er* are even formed; then the *I am*
appears after the event (in this case raising my arm),
and claims that it chose (doership or choosership). In
this way, psychology as the practical arm of philosophy, and philosophy as the handmaiden of theology,
must discard this idea of choice or something could
have happened other than what happened. We must
understand that *we are not separate from nature.* We, as
Spinoza suggests, are not a kingdom within a kingdom, a world within a world. We are one with nature
and made of the same *one substance*, the illusion is that
we are separate from nature.

In India, people say that there are four basic properties that go along with being human as part of nature:
we must eat, we must sleep, we must go to the bathroom, we must have sex. Quantum psychology added
that we have a natural learning response, and we have

a natural merging response. More recently, in the study of animal behavior and anthropology, researchers have discovered that animals, not only human beings, but our closest relatives, the apes, are *social animals*. Therefore, we are not just eating, sleeping, going to the bathroom, having sex, learning and merging, but we are also social animals. What becomes clear is that any deprivation in any of these areas throws the nervous system into a survival or sublimated response.

The nervous system is the great *illusioner*. The nervous system responds to certain stimuli through the senses; the brain *transduces* (*trance*-duces) it and creates an illusion (*trance*) of a self, which has choice, perception, a will, doership, and volition. The key point to understand is that the nervous system omits millions and millions of stimuli and selects only a very small amount (less than 1%), and from that small amount the nervous system constructs the "I," the perceiv<u>er</u>, what the "I" perceives, and what the "I" believes about itself and the world.

The nervous system *trance*-duces sensory information; what the "I" perceives is actually not there, it could be called a hallucination. What you perceive is an abstraction of what is there, an abstraction of less than 1% of what is there (*don't get confused at this point; there is nothing there*). Moreover, the "I," what you call "the self," which is the perceiv<u>er</u> of all of this, is fabricated by the nervous system after the event or action that is perceived has already occurred; *hence, the perceiv<u>er</u> is also an abstraction of* **NOTHING**. This self is a by-product of evolution. The noted geneticist Richard Dawkins, author of *The Selfish Genes*, suggests that the self and consciousness evolved for survival of the species; or as Nisargadatta Maharaj would say, "There is no person . . . the body is made of food" (protein, fats, carbohydrates, etc.). The concept of a self or God is produced by the food body.

THE EVOLUTION OF SELF-CONSCIOUSNESS AND THE ILLUSION OF CONSTANCY

We could say that self-consciousness evolved for two purposes: 1) project an image of a possible future so that we, as part of nature, could survive better, and 2) fabricate the illusion that what "you" perceive is *constant*, stable, permanent, solid, and without the spatial gaps. Spatial gaps occur about 11 to 17 times per second. Consciousness fills in the gaps or space, making the world appear solid, stable, and constant. This is why the two most famous meditations in the last several thousand years are 1) to "find" the *space* between two thoughts, and 2) to "find" the *space* between two breaths.

Consciousness is the vehicle that fills in the gaps of the nervous system's illusions. Within our body, there are literally millions of things happening: blood is circulating, skin cells are dying, new skin cells are forming, etc. There is a constant process going on within the body. The concept of "self" is produced by the body. If there was no body, there would be no concept of self. The illusion that Descartes has is that somehow there is a self that is separate from the body, and this self or soul goes on and on and on. This is also the illusion of spirituality. Call that self "the mind," or call it the "self" or "soul"; but the nervous system selects things out so that we are not aware that cells are dying off all the time and other cells are being born. We are not aware of the fact that more than 90% of one's body consists of fluids, which move, constantly changing; and different things are forming. We are not aware of that. *There is an illusion of constancy. The illusion of constancy ("the illusion of permanence" in Buddhism) means that there is a feeling sense that my hand is always solid and constant.* "I" do not see or experience some cells dying and others being born in a constant movement flowing in and out, things falling off of my body and things coming in. The "I" doesn't see all that or experience all that.

People experience the body as a solid, *constant* whole. In this same way, the self does not experience its changes. It's as if the self is the same self now as it was a minute ago, as it was a year ago. It is because of this *illusion of constancy*, which is created by the brain and nervous system as part of evolution for the purpose of survival. Simply stated, you would not even know you were a separate solid unit if you were constantly aware that you were changing and changing, instant to instant to instant.

Jacques Derrida, the father of postmodern deconstruction, made an interesting statement: "The self is a formation of the suppression of difference." (Coward, *Derrida and Indian Philosophy*, p. 61) This means that language is always being suppressed in speech; this suppression of differences gives the sense of self. Constancy and suppression of difference denies that everything is changing all the time. The illusion of fixedness, the illusion of a solid stable self, creates the experience of a solid self and a solid stable world. This illusionary solid self imagines it has choices, perceives things, is the perceiver of things, wills things. This is the great illusion of the nervous system. In the Buddha's Diamond Sutra he declares, "There is no world."

Descartes mistakenly believed that "I" move my arm, "I" am willing it, "I" am thinking of moving "my" arm and then "I" move "my" arm by my will, choice, and volition. What Descartes could not realize is that the concept of choice arises after the event or action has already taken place. This Cartesian error misses the great illusion of the nervous system; hence, it perpetuates the great illusion of psychology, i.e., the illusion of choice, will and volition.

QUESTION:
Why do many spiritual systems imply that thinking is bad?

"A": Noted philosopher, John Dewey, wrote, "As an organism becomes increasingly complex, its relationship with its environment becomes increasingly uncertain and precarious because as instinct declines as a guide to action, the range of potential actions increases. This produces anxiety. In this way, thought is a biological response to this natural stimulus in a complex organism. Doubt as to what to do next creates a problem and thought arises to resolve the problems that arise, from our relations with out actual and social environment. Such thoughts become intellectual when it actually changes the environment to make it more secure and less precarious."

An organism, i.e., moves from being an amoeba up the Darwinian chain and now we have a human being. Soon the relationship with the environment becomes more uncertain rather than less certain. For amoebae there is no thought process involved. It's very simple. As we become more and more complex, things become more and more uncertain because to an amoeba you either fight, flight, or freeze. To us, there are so many possibilities in the context of that and because of socialization and natural instinct that we have towards fight, flight, freeze or pray it can no longer act as a guide to action. Because we have no real guide any longer to action because socialization and complexity has made things so, that there are many more actions that are possible than fight, flight, or freeze. We can talk, we can get in a car and go someplace. Because there are so many different actions and because instinct is declining, fight, flight freeze or pray as primary guide in our consciousness. We have anxiety because we don't know exactly what to do. Thus, thoughts are the products of our physiological processes; thoughts are produced as ways of responding to all the things that are going on. Therefore, thought is not bad. Thought is a natural response to a complex world because the human organism has lost its instincts, or its instincts have diminished. Instincts are not present in your consciousness all the time. Doubt as to what to do next creates problems. *Thoughts arise in a functional, natural way as an attempt to solve problems in our relationship with our environment.* This is an attempt to change the environment in some way and to make the environment more secure, safer, and less dangerous. *So, all thought, all feelings, and all emotions are natural and functional in that their purpose is to help the organism survive.*

For this reason, "spirituality" and psychology have lost their direction. If you are in India, you are focused on the *Yoga Sutras*, which say, "yoga is the stilling of the thought waves of the mind." You don't want thoughts. Thoughts are somehow bad. Emotional states, other than bliss and love, are bad. And if you're in the Judeo-Christian world, certain thoughts and feelings are "bad" and other thoughts and feelings are not bad. Instead, understand the *naturalistic, functionalistic* way that these things are useful and serve a purpose for a human organism, in a 21st Century context, that is trying to survive.

The problem arises when, and only when, the judgment is placed on this *naturalistic, functionalistic* phenomenon that thoughts are "bad," or emotions are "bad," or certain thoughts are "bad," or are "appropriate" or "inappropriate" when societal standards, judgments, evaluations, and significances are laid upon something: The judgment that certain thoughts and feelings might be bad; the evaluation that somehow it is an evaluation of me, if I have less thoughts I am better than if I have more thoughts, if I have purer feelings, i.e., love and bliss and joy, I am better than if I have anger, hate and sadness; and the significance that one is better than the other. If we contain all of this in the context of *functional and natural, it is a natural phenomena and it is functional in that it enables the organism to try to cope with a very complex environment.* The more complex the organism, the more thoughts, the more choices, the more confusion, the more emotions, etc. These are all attempts at coping or resolving what the external world is naturally presenting to us, so we view that in relation to survival.

Now, let's get back to the initial question.

"A": In the mind narratives we use an imaginary word, "mind," as if this metaphor could be an agent of thoughts, feelings, emotions, associations, perceptions. The "mind" is an abstraction that is produced by the physical body and the nervous system. The mind metaphor is produced by the body, it is not independent of the body, or, as it is said in Middle Way Buddhism, "There is only *dependent arising.*" How could the mind, the "I," and the perceiver of events possibly cause external events, since they are by-products of the body, and they arise after the events have already occurred? Moreover, the concept called *consciousness*, or what the mind is made of, or what the world is made of, must have an "I" (which is a product of language) present to say that a thing called *consciousness* even exists.

"A": On a Roll [The Natural Psychology]
   Spinoza understood and presented the realization that we are part of, not separate from, nature; and as a part of nature, we respond and do as nature does.

"Most writers on the emotions and on human conduct seem to be treating rather of matters outside nature than of natural phenomena following nature's general laws. They appear to conceive man to be situated in nature as a kingdom within a kingdom for they believe that he disturbs rather than follows nature's order, that he has absolute control over his actions and that he is determined solely by himself. They attribute human infirmities and fickleness, not to the power of nature in general, but to some mysterious flaw in the nature of man which, accordingly, they bemoan, deride, despise or, as usually happens, abuse.

He who succeeds in hitting off the weakness of the human mind more eloquently and more acutely than his fellows is looked upon as a seer." (Spinoza, *The Ethics of Spinoza*, p. 23)

Evolution as a Continuum

"A": (continuing): Another part of this naturalistic understanding of nature was to appreciate Nagarjuna's via Buddha's "no separate independent self," evolution can best be illustrated as a continuum. Let's first imagine human beings as a species that is separate and distinct from apes, which is a species distinct from monkeys, which is a species distinct from dogs, which is a species distinct from cats, etc. We have lines separating me from dogs and cats and so on. However, if evolution is a continuum, then every single thing has a common ancestry. It joins us not only to everything, but it also makes us realize quite clearly that we are all part of one another. To illustrate this, apes have 95% to 98% of the same DNA as we do. Evolution is an interconnected process on a continuum.

The nervous system organizes; and under threat it organizes around fight, flight, freeze, or pray. In other words, there is a place that the nervous system goes to in the midst of chaos, whereby the way to organize that chaos and look for meaning in chaos, is through prayer. Prayer, as an organizing principle, is a defensive survival reaction.

Everything is inter-relational. Nature is basically one inter-relational substance. Arthur Schopenhauer would call that the *principle of sufficient reason*, but he took that idea from the Buddha. For the Buddha, everything was inter-related, everything was dependent upon everything else and since everything was dependent upon everything, there was no independent origination. No thing exists in itself, by itself, separate from anything else. Moreover, nothing has a separate, independent self-nature or presence that exists outside of the illusion that language creates.

There can be no separate individual cause and effect, we are not separate from nature. There can only be *one substance* and that *one substance* yields no separate cause and effect because everything is connected to everything else. There is no separate independent self.

On Desires

"A": Desires are for survival. When "I" am tired, "I" desire sleep. When "I" am hungry, "I" desire food. When I have to go to the bathroom, "I" decide to go to the bathroom. Desires are survival-based. When desires are thwarted, stopped, or prevented by society, they become sublimated or substituted. In other words, "I" have a desire for sex. Instead of allowing and having that desire for sex, which "I" cannot fulfill, at age 13, "I" sublimated, and all of a sudden "I" got interested in differential calculus or, "I" substituted, "I" want to sleep. Sometimes "I" have heard people say that because someone doesn't sleep or eat, somehow they are more advanced spiritually. That is spiritual sublimation.

When desires are thwarted or prevented, they become socially sublimated. When they are re-pressed or expressed, their justification becomes the nervous system fabricating an individual self-centered psychology. This means that if the nervous system, through socialization, represses a desire, the experience that emerges from the repression of desire and the ideology or the justification for the repression of the desire becomes "my" psycho-mythology. For example, if "I" have a sexual desire, and, because of socialization, "I" repress the desire, that energy must go somewhere. Now, the energy, according to Wilhelm Reich, goes upward into my head, or we could say metaphorically, the energy goes into the cortex and "I" develop, for example, a spiritual philosophy, and "I" might theorize, "it's good to repress desires," or "the desire for sex is bad." Sex is ignoble in some way; "I" may have a desire for sex with somebody, but "I" am not supposed to desire sex. If "I" express or repress that desire, then "I" develop a psycho-mythology or philosophy to justify that particular action. In other words, in the former, you should express yourself. In the latter, you must give up desire.

Simply stated, you should, etc., etc., etc.

Desires are the motivating factors for survival, and when those desires get sublimated, i.e., expressed or repressed, both of them develop a justification, a reasoning, to justify their expression or repression. In other words a philosophical, psychological-mythological justification is produced. Unfortunately, or fortunately, if the energy of the particular desire is repressed or denied, it becomes aberrated. In other words, let's say I have an incredible desire for food, "I" suppress it, "I" get into sex or religion. Nothing actually gets suppressed. What happens is that it gets suppressed but it *leaks out* in some way. Desires are the body's natural motivation toward survival or, as the noted postmodern philosopher, Gilles Deleuze would say, the body is a *desiring machine*.

CHAPTER 10

RULES

"STRUCTURAL SEED STORY"
There are universal laws that are true in all cases.

"A": In this universal truth claim story, laws and rules have a metaphysics that govern them. Laws and metaphysics are made by individuals who *perceive* things, *deduce* things, and *conclude* things. We could say at best, especially given quantum physics, that we have *probabilities*. If *"I"* pick up a pen and let go, the probability is extremely high that this pen will drop. These are all probabilities. An *"I"* can never say that anything is true in *all* cases. There can't be because there is *no such thing as free will*, the abstracted *"I"* that claims free will arises after the action and event have already happened. Moreover because there is only *one substance*, a droplet of water in the ocean doesn't have a choice about going this way or that way, it's all going in one particular way.

David Hume said that since everything is mediated and is a representation (because it is a perception and an abstraction), *the story and perception of cause and effect too is a representation and an abstraction!!!* Moreover, the story of free will is also a representation, an abstraction.

"STRUCTURAL SEED STORY"
There are reasons for the things that happen.

"A": Those who create narratives of reason never understand that there is no reason (with a capital *R*) that exists outside of the word *reason*. The nervous system produces the concept of reasons after the event or actions have occurred; reasons are abstracted justifications that arise after the action has already occurred. Primitive, infantile understandings reason that "I" was punished and didn't get my treat because "I" did something bad; and if "I" do something good, then "I" get good things. This is an infantile understanding transferred onto the world of spirituality. Reasons for things occurring implies that the *one substance* had some kind of a plan, some kind of design, or some kind of agenda. This story infers a separate "it" that is putting a separate "I" through something; *the substance* is just itself. Reasons are a justification for things that have already happened. For example, "I" met somebody recently who told me that there's always a reason for things that happen because the soul is in an evolutionary process, and that things happen and help the soul to evolve. That implies that everything happens for a purpose, i.e., that it is for the soul's evolution. It implies that there is a soul, something separate from something else. It implies that there is an evolution from *one substance* into another substance. If there is *only one substance*, how can there be a separate individual soul? How can there be an evolution of a soul? How can there be progress, let alone why would there necessarily have to be a reason?

The nervous system likes the story of reasons, so that it can learn how to survive better. If "I" learned that every time "I" touched the stove "I" burn my hand, then "I" now have learned that; and the reason my hand got burned was because "I" touched the hot stove; therefore, I'll survive better if "I" do not. The nervous system produces reasons, and it desires understanding because if it has understanding and reasons then it fantasizes that it can survive better. In general, reasons become socialized and spiritualized rituals of behavior, which demand that an "I" conform to society's rules.

"STRUCTURAL SEED STORY"
Reality is governed by law. Law confirms the cosmos.

"A": In law truth claim narratives, there is some kind of something that governs and rules these rituals. Laws are made by people. *The substance* does not make law, because there is only *one substance*. How can a substance make a law? This universal law story is anthropomorphic. The cosmos is not run by laws. *That substance is that substance is that substance.* Laws arise when the "I" appears, the nervous system creates the story of laws and reasons to understand why things happen the way they happen or don't happen when they don't happen. In short, it is an attempt by the nervous system to organize chaos. There is no Law (with a capital *L*) "up there," which exists outside of the word "law" and the *language game* and linguistic usage that gets fabricated to use such a word.

"STRUCTURAL SEED STORY"
There is total order and you have a place in the universe.

"A": The concept of order and place exists in language only. There is only *the substance*. "Order" implies a hierarchy, and the hierarchy is projected by people onto the substance. In ancient India, we had a caste system. Later, a whole cosmology from gods to angels to people to animals was abstracted. This hierarchy, was accompanied by how we should act within this hierarchy. There is no such hierarchy. You do have a "place," but not a "special place," in the universe in the sense of everything is everything and is made of *the substance*. *The substance* does not have a hierarchy. To say that you have a "place" could be interpreted in a psychological *language game*: if you have a place, then you fit in.

"STRUCTURAL SEED STORY"
Act within your role.

"A": In this restrictive role narrative, act within the order, means act within your role, or act within the hierarchy or act within your position. Each implies a position that you have, and if you act within it, you get to Nirvana. This is a Hindu caste hierarchy, whether it be from gods to angels to people, or through a caste system. If you stay within that hierarchy, if you stay and act within your hierarchy, you'll get a good birth next time. Note that the reincarnation narratives aid in diminishing life experience. In other words, the statement, "it will be better in the next life, or "it's your karma" only suggests that what happens now is not so important, thus helping to diminish pain.

This "acting within your role" can also be likened to the concept of the word *appropriate* in the world of psychology. People will say, well that's not "appropriate" behavior, or this is not appropriate behavior. "Appropriate" is a standard, which becomes a behavioral ritual that is given to people when they are children to describe what is good behavior and what is bad behavior. What is appropriate behavior? Within a system, or discursive structure, it comes from a <u>cultural standard</u>. When you don't act within that "appropriate behavior," you are considered bad, awful, terrible or worse than that, you could be diagnosed as having problems or being mentally ill.

"STRUCTURAL SEED STORY"
Liberation is liberation from our bodily senses.

"*A*": This is a "body is bad" story. It isn't so much giving up the senses, it is more a realization that the experien<u>cer</u> and perceiv<u>er</u> of experiences is produced after the event has already occurred. Moreover the experience occurs after sensations and the perceiver of experience, which is a by-product and abstraction of sensations. So, how can an "I" liberate itself from bodily sensations when the "I" is made of abstracted bodily sensations.

"STRUCTURAL SEED STORY"

If the soul has properly purified itself from its attachment from bodily things, this is called virtue, then after death it will no longer return into bodies but into another world.

"A": *There is no separate individual soul,* so how can it be purified? How could a soul, which came from and is the *one substance* or a de-centered God be other than the *one substance* or God?

When you detach from bodily things such as eating, sleeping, having sex, making money, we call this some kind of virtue. I don't understand; why would it be a virtue?

"STRUCTURAL SEED STORY"

Isn't there such a thing as virtues and vices in morality, or is that nonexistent?

"A": The best way to look at this is through the work of Friedrich Nietzsche, who traced the history of morality. For Nietzsche, originally there were slaves and masters. The slave, in order to survive, had to *develop* survival behaviors; for example, how to be meek, how to be humble, how to be subservient, non-attached, how to be giving and compassionate to the master.

The master, on the other hand, was viewed by *the slave* as full of the seven deadly sins: pride, envy, lust, greed, gluttony, wrath, and sloth. It becomes an interesting twist that the Christian religion, was formulated by slaves. Consequently, "virtues" that are commonly accepted and taught as being closer to God and more godly were the qualities that the slaves had to develop as a way of surviving. The slaves had to learn to be subservient, be humble, be compassionate, and learn how to serve. They had to learn how to be meek; and so the slaves wrote, "the meek shall inherit the earth." And, so this particular understanding, and this way of being became *nobilized* (made noble) and *spiritualized* (made spiritual), and became labeled as virtue by the slaves. The behaviors of the masters were labeled by the slaves as vices: pride, greed, lust, etc. The masters had the money and the slaves did not. Spiritual texts were written by slaves (Jews who became Christians), "It was easier for a camel to go through the eye of a needle than for a rich man to enter into the kingdom of Heaven." And, in this way, the survival defense mechanisms of the slave were spiritualized into virtues, and the behaviors of the masters were made into vices. There is a *genealogy of morals*, according to Nietzsche.

Notice that if we have virtue, then after death, we will no longer return into the pain or slave body, but you will go to another world, or have a better birth.

The soul has fallen into a body because of desires (the master has fallen). Slaves judge themselves and others (the masters) who have bodily desires as not having virtue, the slaves, for survival, defined virtue as giving up bodily desires. Then slaves who had to repress or give up desires for survival reasons came up with the perfect rationale for their behavior; they imagined that if they did give up desires, it was somehow spiritual and they would go to another world or better birth. Nietzsche, in *Beyond Good and Evil*, asks us to go beyond these concepts.

There is no sin or virtue or good or evil, just the *one substance*.

"STRUCTURAL SEED STORY"
Truth leads to freedom.

"A": The concept of *truth* and the concept of *freedom* exist in language only. Nirvana is not freedom, *Nirvana means extinction*, the understanding that *you are not* leads in Buddhism to Sunyata (the **de-void** of **void**) or extinction. This is when the experienc<u>er</u> of the **void** and the **void** is "seen" (forgive the language) as an abstracted representation of **NOTHING**, then the experienc<u>er</u> of the **void** and the **void** vanish (this is **Post-Deconstruction**). The illusion is that Nirvana is this ultimate *feeling* of freedom because freedom implies a state, an experience, as if you can do whatever you want. Liberation leads to *nothing* and even *not nothing* (Sunyata). Nirvana means extinction. Liberation does not mean that you are or become something. Liberation is the "realization" that <u>you are not</u>.

"STRUCTURAL SEED STORY"
If you play the game right, follow God's rules today,
then tomorrow or in the next life, things will be better.

"A": Behavioral truth claims are narratives to get you to behave yourself and be good and docile. It implies a separate God. It implies a game or path. It implies rules. It implies a next life, all of which are not. All of these imply different substances and they presuppose a space-time "I" existence, which is not. It implies ways of being; somehow the "I" will be better off if "it" does them. The question to ask, in light of Nietzsche's slave-master morality, is this: Who is in charge of and decid-

ed the labels of good, bad, sin, and virtue? Also, who legitimizes good, bad, sin, and virtue? And against whose <u>cultural standards</u> are these determined?

"STRUCTURAL SEED STORY"
There are universal rules and morals.

"A": Moral narratives are best exemplified by the renowned philosopher, Emanuel Kant who, as the mouthpiece, proposed a structural seed story that certain things are always right, always good, and that you should act in such a way that your actions would become universal laws. This he called the *categorical imperative.*

There is no such thing as a universal morality or rules of conduct and behavior, or a categorical imperative. How could there be when there is only *one substance*? The abstracted "I" arises, which says this is better than that, or this is a universal good after the event and action has already occurred, and is a judgment by the nervous system, which is made solely for the purpose of its own survival.

"STRUCTURAL SEED STORY"
Through outer ritual (the path), you get to know God.

"A": Nothing the "I" does can get you to God. The concept of "I" and God, as a logos with a location outside the universe, ultimately will dissolve. The "I" has no power. It arises after the event and the action have already occurred; even the abstracted construct of consciousness arises later.

"You" might do a spiritual practice for a while, until "you see" through it as a construct, a story. But, if you are really deeply honest with yourself, and "I" have known so many people who have done spiritual practice for 10, 20, 30 years, who are still in misery in their lives, and yet they never question the fact that maybe they are in misery in their lives because they were given *misinformation* or they were with the wrong guru or path. In this case, the *misinformation* is that they will get to God and get into this existence, this consciousness, this blissful state, for all of eternity and live forever and never be reborn and never have pain and suffering if they do this spiritual practice. It is just not so. There is only *one substance*, and *a de-centralized, nonlocalized God, is that one substance*, as is everything else. But once everything is de-centered, there is no God, substance, or "I," just Nirvana as extinction, which is Sunyata, which is NOT.

"STRUCTURAL SEED STORY"
Confess and be absolved of sin, i.e., tell your truth and you will be forgiven.

"A": In "the sinner confesses and is forgiven" narratives, the addressee (student) is given a mandate: confess and be absolved of sin. This implies that if an "I," which appears after the action is already done, just confesses, then God (the sender or addresser of the information) will forgive "you" for this bad thing "you" imagine "you" did. From the "point of view" of the substance (and I hate to use point of view because it implies it has a point of view), as *the substance*, there is no good or bad or sin or virtue or point of view.

In India, one guru said, "Man is much smarter than God. Man knows all about good and bad, high and low, right and wrong, sin and virtue. God doesn't know anything about that. God just is." Confess and you will be absolved, forgiven by God, implies different substances, and an "I" that arises after the action has already occurred, which imagines that it is the bad doer of the action, should be forgiven for something it did not do.

Recently, the New-Agers said, *tell your truth* and you will be forgiven. "You" and "your truth" is a subjective abstraction of **NOTHING**, and that's all it is.

There is no reason to forgive anyone or not forgive anyone because they did not *do* anything or *not do* anything. What makes it very, very difficult to "be in the world" is that the nervous system projects and then applies man-made spiritual truths, which are complete fabrications, onto *the substance*.

"STRUCTURAL SEED STORY"
*Everything is perfect, therefore there must be
a purpose, plan, or design.*

"*A*": If everything is perfect, why would we need a purpose, plan or design? If everything is the same *one substance*, what or who could imply that something was imperfect, planned or unplanned, designed or undesigned?

Jacques Derrida would say that the word *perfect* would have no meaning without the word *imperfect*. With *one substance* there is neither.

"STRUCTURAL SEED STORY"
Grace (which comes from the Greek work meaning favors),
heals, overcomes disease, weakness, etc., so he who receives
grace can make good choices and overcome sin.

"A": This story implies that if "I" do <u>culturally determined</u> good deeds (good things), then "I" will receive this Grace from some centralized, localized outside source and be able to overcome diseases. This story says that by "my" action, which "I" do, "I" will receive something. This entails a *separate* "I," which alters behavior *as if you have choice* over what "you" do and what "you" don't do. The "I" and the experience of "I" arises after the perceived action and event have already taken place. How could an "I" be a choos<u>er</u> or a do<u>er</u>? How could an "I" receive anything from a separate substance, which is something "outside" of itself? The *one substance* is what everything is made of.

*TEACHERS WHO SAY THERE IS NO "I"
WOULD BE MORE CORRECT IF THEY
SAID THAT NO "I" IS ARISING ("FOR
THEM"); THIS IS A BIOLOGICAL OCCUR-
RENCE, NOT A REASON TO WORSHIP
THEM.*

"A"

"STRUCTURAL SEED STORY"
We must earn Grace.

"A": This "work and earn your place in Heaven" story has the problem that it is a nice idea to say "I" would like to earn Grace, but it leaves the onus and the pressure on an abstracted "I," which comes after the event and action has already happened. How can this "I" choose something which has already occurred, in order to earn this Grace? The "I" itself cannot earn Grace through behavior or choices or repressing some kind of sexual or other desire, since that has already occurred or not occurred before the "I" arises to take blame or praise for the action. You cannot earn Grace, it either occurs or it does not occur.

"STRUCTURAL SEED STORY"
Perseverance is Grace.

"A": The ability to either do a spiritual practice or to go on through painful things is not up to a separate individual "I." There is no separate individual self. In fact, the *Siva Sutras* would even say that during a prayer it is consciousness (*the substance*) that asks and consciousness (*the substance*) that answers the prayer. There is only *one substance*, which appears as two or more substances. There is no individual person with good qualities and/or bad qualities. There is the substance, which appears as different substances to the illusion of separate individual "I"s. The separate individual "I"s are made of *the substance*.

"STRUCTURAL SEED STORY"
Grace is achieved through a conversion experience.

"A": This Calvin-Puritan conversion narrative demonstrates how religions, in this case Protestantism, suggest that you receive this Grace that saves you from death (salvation). You receive the Grace and then you die, and you go to life everlasting. The big question in Christianity is this: How do you know that you are saved (from death)? The answer in this story is that you achieve this through a conversion experience. This story gave rise to the Evangelist movement, particularly in the United States: Protestants try to have this "conversion experience." Contained within the conversion experience, is an "I" which had a conversion experience; therefore, "I" have the Grace[15].

Problems arose because it implies that when you are born, God has already decided that you will be saved and live a life everlasting in Heaven, or that you will be damned to Hell. In this theological story, it is already decided. The only way you can know which way you are going is through a conversion experience. Along with the experience, there is an underlying assumption that once you have this conversion experience, you know that you were the chosen one and you will live a life everlasting and not go to Hell. The problem is the assumption that everything in life will be great after this. There will be no problems. What happens when problems arise, as they will, whether it be

---

[15] The desire to have a "conversion experience" is distantly related to the search for "spiritual" experiences, which is a phase that must be discarded because all "spiritual" experiences require an "I" to experience them.

a car accident or the loss of a job, a loved one gets sick and dies, whatever it may be, the Protestant will then question himself or herself and say "Was it really a conversion experience or did 'I' just *think* 'I' had a conversion experience?" So, this particular idea is laden with assumption upon assumption upon assumption. The first one is that God already decided whether you will go to Heaven or Hell, which presupposes a Heaven and a Hell that are separate from every other substance. The way to find out if "I" am saved is to have the conversion "experience." The last part is, How do "I" know "I" had one? If "I" had this experience, then bad things shouldn't happen, so "did 'I' really have the experience, or did 'I' just *imagine* that 'I' had the experience?"

Another way to get to know whether you will have this conversion experience, if you'll be saved rather than damned, is to do good deeds, work hard; then it will appear in your life and you'll have a family and you will have all these wonderful rules that you'll follow. This would prove that you were saved too. But, of course, the question that always emerges is this: "Am 'I' really feeling like 'I' was converted and had a conversion experience?" "Am 'I' really feeling like 'I' am living a good life, or am 'I' just acting and pretending to have a good life?"

The purpose of grace is to overcome sin. But if there is only *one substance,* there is no sin.

"STRUCTURAL SEED STORY"
Spiritual books and texts are the authority.

"A": Martin Luther suggested that the way you are saved is to hold onto the Gospel, hold onto the sacraments, and hopefully you'll get the Grace and you'll be saved. Spiritual books and texts can give you "understanding," if you are fortunate to find a good one, which is still very difficult because writing any kind of spiritual book or text, you are dealing in language, and language by its very nature is binary (dualistic) descriptive, and slippery. Language by its nature is metaphoric and descriptive. The best that they could do is to give you someone's position or point of view about what they "experienced," but there is still an abstracted "I" that experienced the point of view. Nisargadatta would have said, "Whatever you say it is, it isn't."

"STRUCTURAL SEED STORY"
Everything is in order, coordinated, and in synchronicity and harmony with and by God for a purpose.

"A": "I" wouldn't say everything was "in order" because "in order" implies a structure. There is no ultimate structure. There is no ultimate order. There is no one in control. It is not coordinated for a purpose by some "source" for some reason. There is no synchronicity. Everything is synchronicity, or nothing is synchronicity and everything is in harmony because there is only *one substance*. If everything is synchronistic, then nothing is synchronistic. It's like being in

the ocean saying everything is water. There is *one substance, and there is no substance except in language!!!*

"*R*": Wow!!!

"STRUCTURAL SEED STORY"
Everything has a cause.

"*A*": A separate individual cause implies a separate individual effect, and a separate individual location. Since everything is made of the *same substance*, as everything else, there can be no separate cause and effect. The whole universe causes everything to happen; moreover, there are no separate locations.

To paraphrase Neils Bohr, one of the founders of quantum physics: *to talk about quantum physics we must talk about non-locality.* Everything causes everything else, and everything reaps the effect of everything else. There is no separate individual cause that creates a separate individual effect, or as renowned physicist John Stuart Bell said, "There are no local causes."

"STRUCTURAL SEED STORY"
There is an ultimate source point that causes everything, and it is above us.

"*A*": Whether the source point is above us or the source point is within us, it still represents a point in spacetime and a source_r_, or self that has an origin (beginning) and a location. Since there is only *one substance*, there can't be that which sourc_es_ something other than itself. There is no source or sourc<u>ee</u> separate from itself. There is no source because there is no sourc<u>er</u> or originator, sourcing or originating things. There is only *that one substance.* There is no beginning, moreover, the words "source," "origin," "beginning," and "cause" exist in language only. There is no source, origin, beginning, or cause outside of language.

"STRUCTURAL SEED STORY"
There is good and evil.

"A": Good and evil implies two substances, and in Nietzsche's *Genealogy of Morals,* the good and evil is determined by the slave. Good and Evil exist in the perceiv<u>er</u> and in language only, and they exist only within a specific referential system. There is only *one substance,* not good or evil. An abstracted "I" has created the "good" and "evil" constructs. Good and evil exist in language only.

"STRUCTURAL SEED STORY"
*Pain is compensated for. If you have faith,
then you get an eternity of bliss.*

"A": This pay (with pain) now and receive bliss later narrative, or no gain without pain, or pain-is-an-opportunity-for-growth reframe is a mythology to explain life's contradictions. This is the Christian martyr story, a spiritual reframe that is silly at best, and a defense against no center, source, location, or originary presence at worst.

CHAPTER 11

SPIRITUAL AND/OR CULTURAL LIFESTYLES

"STRUCTURAL SEED STORY"

One should emulate or imitate the life of saints and teachers.

"A": This infantile fusion story is based on the idea that if the abstracted "I" acts like this, and if an abstracted "I" behaves like that, and if an abstracted "I" does this, then an abstracted "I" will get to Heaven or some kind of reward. Usually this involves chastity, piety, fasting, meditating, or some kind of "spiritual or cultural lifestyle." So, what happens is, *we are looking at the outer actions of an abstracted "I," which arises after the action and event have already occurred as a way to get a state, i.e., heaven or Nirvana.* Or, the actions of an abstracted "I," who believes it can control, cause, or bring about a certain desired result. The abstracted "I" appears after the action and event has already taken place, and the "I" appears with the state. It is only "later" that the abstracted "I" comes up with ways to justify or try to reason out a way to bring about a different state.

It is very difficult for people to grasp that the abstracted "I" and, hence the abstracted "I"'s *psycho-mythology* called psychology, exists in language only. You can process and process and process on a psychological level, it is still a *language game!* The abstracted "I" and the illusion of doership and its psychological *language game* arises after the actions and events have already occurred. This is the problem with psychology. Volition, choice, action, and experience has already occurred by the time the abstracted "I" perceives it. *THE "I" IS PAST TENSE!! THE ABSTRACTED "I" IS PAST TENSE!* Psychology created a whole framework of language, words, and concepts, which is a structure that makes sense within the *language game.* The *language game* is a tautology, and it is a structure that determines everything within its own *language game,* but not outside of it.

Psychological diagnoses exist in language only, in theories, not necessarily in people. The question to ask is, "Who produced and determines these diagnostic labels?" And since it is produced by abstracted "I"s, which arise after the action or event, why would the "I"'s abstracted description be valid?

"STRUCTURAL SEED STORY"
You should conduct your life in such a way as to attain salvation.

"*A*": Spiritual paths are spiritual and cultural *language games.* They suggest the following: don't be angry, don't be lustful, don't be sad, don't be greedy, be loving, be a vegetarian. Tighten up all of your orifices and then you'll get saved. In the Christian sense, "saved" means that you will not die. You will live life everlasting with Christ, God, or in some other universe, or in Heaven, which is mistakenly called Nirvana. In the Hindu sense, you can go to Heaven (Vaikunta) or get a better birth. This is a resistance to death; simply put you don't have to die. In these stories, you're asked to live a spiritual (cultural) lifestyle for which we give up freedom, i.e., What we can eat or do, feel, etc.; and we are given the concept that if "I" give up "my" freedom, which is reframed as surrender, and *become docile*, play the game, and serve the guru, a *centralized* God, then he or she will give "me" freedom. As mentioned earlier, the slave morality of Nietzsche becomes spiritualized as noble and virtuous rather than being seen as a slave's survival strategy. Moreover, the social, political, and spiritual system insists that we become *docile*. This attempt to make people docile occurs during socialization, and is reframed later in psychological *language games* as "acceptance." But the unspoken discourse, according to Michel Foucault, is that the authorities, spiritual teachers, psychologists, etc., are there to help you *become docile*, and supports the social structures in power.

"STRUCTURAL SEED STORY"
The number of people that follow you around is equal to the amount of virtue you possess.

"A": This story is very guru or teacher related.

"R" to **"A"**: "I" remember being told by a friend that in about 1982, he spent a few weeks with with *Satya Sai*

*Bab*a. "He" would see people and ask them, "What is this guy, does he have anything?" People would reply, "He has to, because there are so many people here."

"A" to "R": This, Friedrich Nietzsche would call the herd mentality. On a neurological level, a brain level, there is a survival mechanism called "following the herd." I will survive better if I follow the herd of people. Imagine horses; they have a leader in the herd called a stallion, and the horses go where this stallion goes because the species has survived better when the herd followed a stallion. Most people follow the herd. They go along with what everyone else does, never questioning. Now you can say that they are sheep. You also could say that on a neurological level, this is a survival-based reaction, which has been passed down genetically for eons. It has nothing to do with the virtue of a teacher or the person or the leader. It is a hardwired, certain, automatic survival response, "'I' will survive better if I follow the leader."

"R": (Nods.)

"STRUCTURAL SEED STORY"
Man was chosen by God.

"A": The seed story, that man is the center of the universe, demonstrates a narcissism within the abstracted "I." Initially the church imagined that the earth was the center of the universe. Then Galileo was excommunicated when he proclaimed that the sun, not the earth was the center of the solar system. For this he

was forced to denounce his own scientific work and he was put under house arrest because it destroyed the Catholic Church's GRAND seed story, which they called church doctrine.

It is narcissistic of the "I" to think that "it" is the center of the universe; moreover, that your spiritual process and growth, or the earth is the center of God's universe, and that God out there gives "you" lessons to learn and opportunities so "you" can grow and join him.

When there is only *one substance*, how could this possibly be going on? Ecclesiastes said, "To think that your life amounts to much is the vanity of vanities."

Noted philosopher and historian, Michel Foucault, said that the discursive structure (in this case the Church's seed story), is controlled and determined by who has the power (in this case the church). The people with the power control the discourse, i.e., what can be said, who can say it, what can be thought, and what is allowed for discussion. With this understanding, it is easy to see how churches, ashrams, psychologies, politicians, and spiritual leaders control the discourse because they are given the power.

"STRUCTURAL SEED STORY"
It is our purpose and the purpose of life to know God.

"A": All *purpose* narratives break down when there is only *one substance*. Purpose-of-life stories presuppose that life has a separate existence and a purpose, because you could be "off" purpose or "on" purpose. But there is only *one substance*, and no separate individual

"you" can be "off" or "on" purpose since there is *one substance*. Most recently, many people have been talking about a mission, a mission statement, their vision, or their "gift." All of these imply that their gift or mission comes from God or is aligned with God. Missions, purposes, gifts, and visions are made up by people, not by a *de-centered, non-local God*, which has no location.

"R": WOW again.

"STRUCTURAL SEED STORY"

*Every time you realize a causal connection,
you make progress.*

"A": This psychological *language game* is a psycho-spiritual misnomer. The search for a cause is the same habit as searching for a logos. This story implies cause and effect. Given the fact that there is only *one substance*, there is no separate individual "you" to isolate one specific cause, which creates one specific isolated effect. *Cause and effect are abstractions that exist in language only.*

The second thing is progress. How could "you" become something other than what you are. If there is only *one substance*, how can there be anything other than the *one substance*. The implication is that "you" can progress and become more than you are right now.

"R": The great misfortune in psychotherapy has been the confusion that insight is the goal of psychotherapy. Insight is not the goal, *change is the goal*. The lan-

guage game of psychology suggests that insight equals change. It's like the old story of the man who went into therapy because he was overweight and depressed. Ten years later, a friend asked him about his progress in psychotherapy. He said, "I'm still overweight and depressed, but now I know *why*."

"STRUCTURAL SEED STORY"
Disease arises because of your past sins.

"A": This narrative seed story implies a past, a present, and a future. *Time is an abstraction that exists in language only*, there is no such thing as time outside of the word "time." And there is no such thing as time if there is only *one substance.*

The concept of "sin" implies that there is a good and bad, a high or low, a right or wrong, a vice or virtue, when there is not because there is only *one substance*. These are only stories. The difficulty when this sin story is believed is that people imagine that if "you" behave in certain ways, then you are "virtuous," and more spiritual and closer to God and good things will happen, and if "you" do things that are "sinful," then you are further away from God and less spiritual and bad things will happen. Therefore, in order to get to Heaven (enlightenment), do good things. The question always has to be, "What referential or cultural system or *language game* are you using to define sin or virtue, good deeds or bad deeds?"

The "I" is an abstracted representation, which exists in language only and arises after the action and event has already occurred, and grants itself doership, agency, or authorship for what has already past. The claim of doership, blame, or praise is assumed by an "I" who was non-existent at the time of the action. *The "I" is past tense.*

"STRUCTURAL SEED STORY"
Deny undisciplined emotions.
Never be controlled by passion.

"*A*": In India, certain emotions are called the five enemies; anger, lust, greed, enmity, jealousy, which are labeled as bad. The good things are love, joy, bliss, etc. The nervous system (of the food body) organizes in such a way that pleasant things, like feelings of love and joy, feel good because they help us in our survival. Bad feelings like anger, hatred, or fear are unpleasant to the nervous system (food body) because, we imagine that they don't help our survival.

The tendency is to spiritualize these good feelings of love, joy, etc., by saying that they are Holy, Godly, or that they came from God and that people who possess these feelings are more spiritual and closer to God. In this way, the first word in the binary is privileged over the second term: *love/hate*. If all is *the substance*, then why or how could *love* be better or closer to *the substance* than the second term *hate*? Religions operating out of survival, teach anger, fear, etc., are bad, and are not spiritual. We should seek and have only the good feelings. Most of spirituality is about pleasure seeking, it's seeking pleasurable experiences such as love, joy, bliss, etc. It is the seeking of pleasant or pleasurable feelings, and calling them spiritual qualities.

The great philosopher, Spinoza, said that all of humanity is like nature. The "negative" emotions are as *natural* as are the positive ones. In Part Three of his *Ethics*, Spinoza presents an analysis of emotions as natural processes, without judgment. When they are held or understood in this light, they are "accepted" and lose much of their charge.

"STRUCTURAL SEED STORY"
There is a fatal flaw within us; call it original sin, or whatever, which must be overcome.

"A": This fatal flaw story, that there is something basically wrong with us, comes initially from the ancient Greeks and their stories or tragedies. This tendency is a way to blame the victim (they have a fatal flaw) so as to gain control.

Aristotle even works out a catharsis for our fatal flaw:
1. Purgation
2. Purification
3. Clarification

Notice how neatly, the fatal flaw narrative has been used for some 2,200 years to reframe pain as an opportunity for spiritual growth.

Quantum psychology discussed a false core, but the false core was an assumption. it is not real. *They are false*; hence, false core. "Sin" implies something really big that is real, and which you must overcome. If it was called "false sin" maybe people would not take it so seriously. The question is, if God is all-good, all-knowing, all-powerful, all-loving, then why would "you" be born with this flaw? And if "you" say, "Well, *'I'* have this fault, it's *my* fault, it's something that *'I'* did wrong," then the question "you" must ask is this: "If there is only *one substance*, could 'I' do something wrong without everything in the universe going along with it?" On a biological level, the "I" cannot choose to do wrong, since it arises after the action has already occurred.

Nature is *one*. We are all made of the same stuff. Each of us is a collection of chemicals. Spinoza said, "They conceive man to be situated in nature as a kingdom within a kingdom; for they believe he disturbs nature, that he has control over his actions ... they attribute human infirmities not to the power of nature, but to some mysterious flaw in the nature of man, which they bemoan, deride, despise and abuse themselves as if they are not part of nature." (Spinoza, *The Ethics of Spinoza*, p. 23)

"STRUCTURAL SEED STORY"
It is spiritual and noble to see beyond life.

"*A*": "I" assume that this story of the "spiritual" is something like this: If you are good, compassionate, loving, and sincere, then these are spiritual qualities; and if you are greedy and lustful, then they are unspiritual. If you are really attached to the earth, in getting and having, then you are evil and bad and unspiritual; and if you're not, then somehow you are good. But the question is, *"What is really spiritual?"*

If *there is only one substance, is there such a thing as spiritual?* Wouldn't it be fairer to say that there is no such thing as spiritual? If Nirvana means extinction, then *there is no Nirvana!!!* No "I," no qualities, no attributes.

Nirvana means extinction; spiritual in most systems means "getting." It is all **NOTHING**, or better said, it is not even **NOTHING**. "Spiritual" implies that there is something unspiritual and less than, which implies different substances. There is no spiritual outside of the word "spiritual." No spirituality exists outside of language. Since there is only *one substance*, there is nothing inherently spiritual or unspiritual. "I am" sorry if you no longer feel special for your spirituality. Maybe we should call spirituality, *"speciality,"* and expose it for what it often is.

"STRUCTURAL SEED STORY"
Self-examination inoculates you from misfortune and pain.

"A": This is one of the great misconceptions in the stories of psychology and spirituality (*speciality*). Somehow, if "I" understand "myself," or if "I" do enough spiritual practice, then nothing bad will happen. We have a very dear friend of ours who is certainly a very sweet, compassionate, loving accepting human being who was a priest for many years. He followed the Christian path for most of his life. Suddenly, his stepdaughter was murdered. He went through a great spiritual crisis because he believed that spiritual and psychological insights protect you from calamity. This shows that there is some kind of incredible belief that somehow, by doing spiritual or psychological practice, all of life's pains will be handled. Moreover, if we examine the plight of the cherished Tibetan people, it is clear that all the "spiritual" practice did not save them from the Chinese.

In the spiritual *language game*, many people who do spiritual practice are told that if they meditated, chanted, did service (Karma, Yoga), that their lives would be handled. It would be an easy life, with an easy job; everything would go great.

In psychology's *language game*, it is assumed that if you know "yourself," then nothing bad will happen; or bad things happen because you are unaware of your psychological structures; or that illness occurs because of psychology. But people who make this assumption do not understand that psychology arises from, and is an abstraction of, biology, not the other way around. "You" could say that since psychology arises after the event or action has occurred, then psychology is not only an abstraction, its meaning is always already deferred, postponed, late, and as an abstraction it is a metaphor at best, and a fiction at worst. Presently, there are even some therapies suggesting that if you change your psychology or frame of reference or strategies; then your illness will disappear.

Spiritual practice has nothing whatsoever to do with the worldly success. The old Zen saying, "Before enlightenment, chop wood and carry water; and after enlightenment, chop wood and carry water," means that you are doing the same things. It is just that the "space" in which you move and do these things is quite transformed. When "you" realize *the substance*, it doesn't mean that you stop going to the bathroom, become a vegetarian, or have only good, sweet thoughts and emotions.

In many spiritual traditions, they promote celibacy as an important thing. Brahmacarya, which means moving or living in Brahma (the substance), in modern times, has mistakenly come to mean celibacy. In India, it is said that life is about eating, sleeping, going to the bathroom, and having sex, or making enough money to get a better place to do it in. If these are *biological functions*, why would it be holy or spiritual to alter your diet, have less sex, or sleep less? It would be like saying that if you went to the bathroom less, then somehow you have a better chance of becoming enlightened.

"STRUCTURAL SEED STORY"
Worship of God saves you from pain and death.

"A": With a centralized, localized God as savior narrative, the centralized God saves you from death. Worshiping God will not save you from pain, death, or bad life events. Great saints like Ramana Maharishi, Ramakrishna Paramahansa, and Sri Nisargadatta Maharaj, all had cancer. Realization does not save you from physical illnesses nor does it save you from death.

Religions are created out of a resistance to dying. Nobody wants to face the fact that they will die, disappear, and it will be as if they never were. Religion does this through taking on the reincarnation story, a soul's evolution, or being saved by Jesus and you will get life everlasting. All of these are resistance to death and they diminish the pains of life. They are stories, nothing more.

"STRUCTURAL SEED STORY"
*All that happens to you is due to your past
bad or good actions.*

"A": In these "It's 'your' fault narratives," if "you" get sick or something bad happens, then it's your fault; i.e., in the psychological *language game*, you should have been aware of it; or in the spiritual *language game*, it is karma or lessons. Let's imagine that a child is born with multiple sclerosis. A child, of a mother who had AIDS, is born with AIDS; or it was born a crack-head; or a child is born with a deformed limb; or a child is born with one ear. The child didn't do anything. If you were born into a family with a history of cancer, and you happen to get cancer, then is it because of your actions, or is it because we need, and religion and psychology needs, reasons or justifications for cause and effect in order to give them some semblance of control and order over what is happening in life. These are cultural *mythologies*, which, according to Claude Levi-Strauss, explain life's contradictions. These stories, as well as the "I" that claims action and doership, arise after the events have taken place—they are fabricated mythologies to organize chaos. They are abstractions and they should be discarded.

"STRUCTURAL SEED STORY"
If you become conscious of things you can control things.

"A": This is both a psychological and a spiritual story. If you are spiritual you can control your diet, you can control your sleep patterns, control your breath, some-

how you could control things. If this were true, then why did all those great teachers (Ramana Maharishi, Ramakrishna Paramahansa, and Sri Nisargadatta Maharaj) who "I" mentioned earlier, have cancer?

In the psychological *language game*, it is assumed that if people become conscious of the past, and conscious of things, then somehow they can control their lives. However, for some people who became involved in psychology, 20 years later, they are still struggling with relationships with their mother and father, and they are still miserable, no matter how conscious they become of things. They don't accept that there is little *causal* connection or correlation between being insightful about their memories of the past and being able to reduce their interpersonal conflicts in the present (i.e., *cause and effect* is a perception and, as such, it is an abstraction). Spiritual and psychological *language game*s are a map, an abstraction, a story, which is a representation of less than 1% of the information that the nervous system can digest, and the representation was produced to organize chaos.

Through therapy, there is an illusion of more choice and more options. But the nervous system on a biological level produces an "I"—choos<u>er</u> after the event and action have already happened. The "I" believes it has choice over this or that. The concept of choice and perception, and perception of choice and volition are representations, abstractions. Therefore, the concept of choice must be discarded.

"R": "I" once asked Nisargadatta Maharaj, "In 1975 I had this satori "experience" in which "I" realized that there was no such thing as choice. Everything that was

to happen would happen and everything that was not to happen would not happen. There was no such thing as choice, is this true?" Maharaj looked at me as if I were a moron, and he said, "Obviously."

"STRUCTURAL SEED STORY"
You can overcome things and become a superman
or a perfected person and achieve perfection and virtue.

"A": This perfection of self or self-growth narrative is a *language game*. If the self or "I" exists as an abstraction in language only, then why or who becomes Nietzsche's "superman"? If there is only *one substance*, how could an abstracted nonexistent "I" be perfected when it appeared by fluids coming together in the brain?

"STRUCTURAL SEED STORY"
Misery and suffering are necessary for self-knowledge.

"A": This is a self-knowledge *language game*. In this story, suffering is seen as an opportunity presented by the universe. If self-knowledge exists in language only, then why would suffering and misery be *necessary* for self-knowledge, except within the context of that *language game*? You might get suffering and misery and still be miserable, and then you might go beyond it, or you may not; but the word "necessary" implies a "must," and this is the error. Moreover, the *perception* of a world "out there" is nervous-system produced, and as the Buddhist Diamond Sutra states, "There is no world."

"STRUCTURAL SEED STORY"
*Somehow you can work on yourself to perfect
the body and become immortal.*

"A": Religious stories are formed for the purpose of resisting the story of death. There is some kind of belief
in most religions that if you are good, perfect, do some
practice, then you will live forever in a better situation,
place, space or beyond, such as a Walden III. In legend
there is even a *siddhi* (power) that you develop in yoga:
if you perfect your body, you can live forever, you can
live thousands and thousands of years. I don't know
why we want to. It would be better to inquire, "By believing this, what are you not wanting to know about
or experience?"

"STRUCTURAL SEED STORY"
Everything is possible.

"A": These omnipotent narratives are put together in
psychological *language game*s by infantile adults who
have fused with magical mommy's or daddy's imagined omnipotence and grandiosity.

Recently there has even been a series of books
written about "infinite possibilities." This is the classic confusion of levels. At the "level" of *the substance*,
everything is possible; but not everything is possible
for an "I" that manifests after events and actions have
already occurred. *The "I"-perceiver is past tense.* There
are infinite possibilities for *that one substance*, but how
it does manifest has nothing to do with "me" because

the "I"-perceiver does not arise until after the events and actions have already taken place. In other words, the "I" comes from *the substance,* it does not come from "me," because the "me" experience is "later."

There is another closely related omnipotent narrative story called "I" co-create with God. In this psychological *language game,* the "I" is equal to God, *the substance.* This narcissistic, egocentric position implies that there is an "I" separate from *the substance,* and a logo-centered God separate from *the substance.* But even if we say there is a logo centered or de-centered God, the "I" that says "I" co-create or "I" create, still comes neurologically after the events and actions have already arisen. *The "I" has no power. There is no "I" as a doer with a separate will or volition.* The "I" appears after the actions and choices have occurred.

"STRUCTURAL SEED STORY"
*If we all progress and do spiritual practice,
it will lead to an enlightened world.*

"A": This is an omnipotent narrative that was once a part of Transcendental Meditation (T.M.); and in an indirect way, it was a misunderstanding of the Buddhist Bodhisattva, which has become the Bodhisattva of narcissism. Recently "I" met someone who said, "I am a Bodhisattva." "I" am going to incarnate again and again and again to help other people become enlightened." This statement implies that there is an "I" separate from *the substance,* that the "I" has will and volition. It implies that there is a thing called "enlightenment"; and to say, "I am going to do all these things,"

when actually, it is *the substance* either contracting or not contracting in such a way as to produce or not produce particular experiences and/or events. It has nothing whatsoever to do with an "I" because the "I" arises after the events and actions have already happened. If you are a Buddhist, then all "you" need to know is *The Heart Sutra*; "Form becomes emptiness, emptiness becomes form: Form is none other than emptiness; emptiness is none other than form." *THERE IS NO BUDDHA or Buddha nature that exists outside of language.*

To live like a Bodhisattva is a technique, a vehicle to annihilate the self by giving and service, not an actual thing that a "you" becomes or and "I" becomes.

In T.M., which became popular in the late 1960s, there was the story that if enough people meditate, then the vibrations of the planet will be changed. Notice that there is more war, more upheaval, more starvation, more pollution, and more meditation.

There is a genetic food body struggling as world population expands and resources for survival shrink! This is a classic confusion of levels. If meditation works to "calm you down" that's great; but to imagine that if enough people do it, the world will be calmed down, implies an "I," which has arisen after the fact, which imagines that it has power over the world, and if enough "I'"s could have enough power over the world, then there would be a peaceful, utopian Walden III. The perception of a world comes from an "I," a perceiver that arises after the event has occurred. It is *the substance* that is "prior" to the arising of the "I."

"STRUCTURAL SEED STORY"
Liberation is to be free of bodily senses.

"A": Liberation is to be free to know that what the eyes see, the ears hear, the voice speaks, are not "me."

Thought is an abstraction of sensation, and thought gives structure and the appearance of order to sensation on a biological level. By doing so, thought and the "I" receive billions of stimuli per second, and can abstract, use or deduce less than 1% of the stimuli. This means that less than 1% of the information received can be taken in by an "I," used, perceived, and realized.

The problem with the "free from the senses" story is that it implies that the senses are bad; here we get back into the Seven Deadly Sins: vanity, jealousy, lust, greed, envy, wrath, and gluttony, which are labeled as bad, when actually they are part of nature.

Fundamentalist Christianity even goes so far as to suggest that the Devil works through the vehicle of sex; and in a more subtle way, in India the devil that confuses and deludes is called Maya.

"STRUCTURAL SEED STORY"
Guru, God, or Jesus takes us beyond suffering and death.

"A": Everything is made of <u>*That one substance*</u>; when you die, you are not. This is the most difficult thing for people to appreciate. As the comedian George Carlin said, "People believe there is this invisible man floating in the sky who watches and keeps count of everything you do, and if you do these good ten things,

you will go to Heaven, and if not, you will go to Hell to burn for all of eternity; but He loves you. These are primitive beliefs."

When you die, *you are not.* People cannot bear that they will not *be* anymore; and to resist this they come up with religious ideas: that they are going to go on somehow forever.

"STRUCTURAL SEED STORY"

*Since I am God, and God created everything,
then I create reality, meaning that if you have
the wrong belief then things go wrong.*

"A": This omnipotent narcissistic narrative is a little bit more on the fairy tale, New Age structure side. You are the *one substance.* If we were to call the *one substance* a non-local, de-centralized *God,* we could say that everything is made of the same substance and that substance could be called *God.* People misunderstand when they believe that since "I" am God, and God creates everything, therefore "I" create everything. The problem is that when the "I," which has awareness and is aware of itself, says "I am God," this "I" statement does not arise until "after" the doing has already happened. If there is only *the substance, as the one substance, there is no "I," no awareness, no anything.* There is no "create," no "not create," you don't even know, there is no "you." When *the substance* contracts and the "I" appears, the "I" says "I am" God, or now "I" created it. The "I" imagines <u>it is</u>. This "I" "experiences" *the substance* rather than no *"I," which is the substance.* This "I," which is aware of itself as separate from the substance and de-

clares "I" created it, is an abstraction that exists in language only and arose after the doing has happened, and it has no power. *It is ego*, because this "I," which arises after the action or events occur, takes blame or praise for something it did not do.

There was once a group of "spiritual" people who said they could create the reality that they wanted. "I" asked them, "How did you know that you wanted it? Because *as the substance*, you wouldn't even know what 'want' or 'not want' even means." Only as an "I," which was separate *from the substance*, would you say, "I" prefer this or that. *As the substance*, there is no "you" to create, because **YOU ARE NOT**. The "I," which comes "later," i.e., "I" want this or that, or "I" created this or that, along with the delusional fantasy that if "I" have the wrong belief, then this is why things go wrong, is a subset of this "'I' create reality" magical fantasy.

This "I" appeared long after the action or event. The "I" "later" determines what "right" and "wrong" are, and later determines that things go right or wrong because of a belief that was "bad" or not "good." The belief concerning why you did what you did is further abstracted, less accurate, comes after the "I," and only acts as a justification or rationale for what occurred. It is a control issue; if "I" control any thoughts or beliefs, "I" control the world.

Soon people who follow this strategy attempt to change the belief. The problem is, the "I" is an abstraction and exists in language only, or as Ludwig Wittgenstein said, *"All problems exist in language only"!!* These beliefs and concepts are abstractions of abstractions of abstractions. *As the substance, there is no "I."* When the

"I" appears, it fabricates that things are "good" and "bad," "right" and "wrong," and "high" and "low." That same "I" now fabricates this: "**Ah!** The reason things were bad was because "I" had this belief, and **Ah!** If I change this belief, then everything will be great." All of these come not *as the substance*, but with the story of the "I." There is only *one substance. The "I" is the substance*, but with self-consciousness it experiences itself as separate from *the substance*; hence at "best," the "I" or "awar<u>er</u>" perceives *the substance* as **void**. As *the substance*, the "I" disappears and the **void** disappears, thus there is no "I" or no "me," which can be termed *samadhi*. Once the "I" appears, you think you are, then all the problems start.

"STRUCTURAL SEED STORY"
Once the flesh is purified, it becomes perfect and becomes God.

"*A*": The body is made of food (protein); the "I" is a by-product of food (proteins). You already are the *one substance*. There is no thing that needs to be purified or needs to become anything.

"STRUCTURAL SEED STORY"
Human beings enjoy divine protection in proportion to their moral perfection and religious piety.

"*A*": This protection story says: "God is up there." "The Lord loves the ones who loves the Lord." If you don't love the Lord, he doesn't love you. This implies not only different substances, but it also implies that the more you love God, the more moral you are, then the more he loves you. Not only does he love you, but he gives you his protection. A non-local, de-centralized God (*the substance*) loves everyone equally, in the same way that the sun shines on everyone equally. In this story, wouldn't a non-local de-centralized God (*the substance*) love everyone unconditionally, regardless of what they do? The question is, What is love? Nisargadatta Maharaj said, "When I experience myself as everything, that is love."

"STRUCTURAL SEED STORY"
Thinking something is almost the same as doing something. If you confess your sins, you will be forgiven and saved, not damned to hell and more pain.

"A": Why should an "I" confess to a sin the "I" could not commit? There is no "I" which does, there is only *one substance*. If the "I" arises and claims doership regarding a sin it did not commit, why should we forgive it, and why would it be saved or go to hell? All of these mistakenly imply different substances, and an "I" that is made of an independent separate substance, which has control, volition, and choice.

IS IT A CULTURAL LIFESTYLE
OR IS IT SPIRITUAL?

*Most "teachers" and students confuse
cultural behaviors and rituals with spiritual
practise like finding out who you are.*

*Cultural behaviors and rituals in India
like arranging marriages, taking off your
shoes, separating men from women,
or male dominated "spiritual" systems are
misconstrued as somehow spiritual
rather than cultural artifacts, particularly
when "teachers" support these behaviors.*

*Unfortunately, the list of cultural rituals
and behaviors mistakenly identified by gurus
as "spiritual" are painfully passed-on to
students desiring to find out who they are.*

*Deconstruction must be clarified by the
"teacher" so that cultural values, behaviors,
and rituals including psychological attitudes,
as well as emotional or dietary inhibitions
are not confused as somehow part of a
"spiritual" practice. Otherwise, students will
take-on part of a cultural baggage
imagining it is spirituality. This taking-on
of cultural behaviors and rituals imagining
it is spiritual is a distraction from direct
confrontation leading to deconstruction. This
gets in the way of finding out who you are
thus prolonging pain.*

"A"

CHAPTER 12

THE MYSTERY

"STRUCTURAL SEED STORY"
Hidden forces are behind events.

"A": In hidden forces metaphors[16], an "I" perceiver, which cannot process more than 1% of its perceptions, calls it a "mystery" as if there is some mysterious force behind things.

The substance is what everything is made of. There are no mysterious forces with plans, intentions, lessons, or an agenda; everything is *the substance*. If everything is made of the ocean, then that is what the waves and water droplets are made of. There is no hidden agenda.

The "danger" in the hidden forces story is that it gives an air of mystery where there is none, and it tends to lead to stories of mysterious forces with mysterious motives, unknown agendas, "mysterious are the ways of the Lord," and hidden purposes. Keep it simple, *one substance*.

---

[16] Hidden Forces metaphors relate to Dark Matter Archetypes. See *The Way of the Human, Volume III*, Chapter III.

"STRUCTURAL SEED STORY"
There are no accidents. Everything has meanings,
purposes; all are lessons from God.

"A": There are no accidents, everything happens because, in order for anything to happen, the entire universe must go along with it. There are no hidden meanings. Meanings are created by a nervous system that is driven to order its perceived chaos. Everything occurs or does not occur. The "I" and perceiv<u>er</u> (which perceives less than 1% of the stimuli that impinges on it determines meaning) arises after the event and actions have already happened. Then this pinprick "I" fabricates meanings, reasons, and purposes.

"STRUCTURAL SEED STORY"
Things just happen or they don't happen,
and these are lessons from God.

"A": This implies that God is a separate substance that will teach something to a separate "I" (which is made of the same substance).

This, in the psychological *language game*, is a classic age regression. Imagine a child that goes to school to learn lessons; and there is a purpose and reason for everything. The nervous system strives to maintain order in its perceived chaotic world by projecting these age-regressed states and a centralized, localized Mom or Dad onto a de-centralized non-localized God or *the substance* and into its religion and spiritual practice.

"STRUCTURAL SEED STORY"

*The source of evil is free will. Thy will, not my will,
oh Lord.*

"A": This story implies an "I" with a will, and that
there is a separate centralized Lord, which has a will.
There is no separate individual Lord; there is no separate individual will; there is no good or evil; and there
is no "many substances," there is *only one substance.*

The "I" claims there is free will; however, the "I"
arises after the action has already happened. There is
only *the substance. Thy will, not my will,* is an affirma-
tion. As in affirming that it is only *by the substance* or
not by the substance, and there is no "me." But to have a
separate Lord with the attribute of a will, an "I" who is
praying to the Lord, "that is the Lord's will," is a frame
of reference to be discarded.

"A" (continuing): Events and actions have already occurred before the "I" arises and perceives it. This why
the existential philosopher, Martin Heidegger, used the
expression, *"thrown into the world or your thrownness."*
In an attempt to verbally convey this "experience," explaining Heidegger in terms of science (1927) is to understand science (2003). The "I" arises and perceives
an event or action *after* it has already taken place. The
"I" feels *thrown into the world* and, in a way, this is accurate because the "I" is formed neurologically after the
event or action occurs as chemicals in the brain come
together. To resist this *"thrownness,"* an entire fictitious,
fabricated, abstracted psycho-mythological *language*

game happens spontaneously, and then the "I" takes credit, blame, or praise for it's imagined psychological creation, which it (the "I") had nothing to do with.

More importantly, Heidegger showed that existence precedes presence (essence). This overturned Plato, who imagined that an essence may be a soul of a thing or presence "up there" that preceded existence. In other words, before Heidegger (1927), it was believed, via Plato (about 400 B.C.), that there was a presence, an essence, a prototype from which existence got its beingness. Heidegger, and later, Sartre, revised this by clarifying that *existence precedes presence or essence, not essence or presence preceding existence!!* It is crucial to understand this!!

Many New Age teachers still profess this soul of the thing or person, even claiming that this soul of an imagined "you" makes agreements before it came to earth. This ridiculous assumption is based on a soul or some essence without a nervous system that comes here to learn lessons. Hopefully, it can be understood that existence (the I AM), through the vehicle of the nervous system, "produces" this "essence" or "soul of the thing" concept, not the other way around.

"STRUCTURAL SEED STORY"
There is a source that has a location and an origin.

"A": Stories about a separate, centralized God in a specific location is a *language game* that gives a centralized God a location and origin, which is transcendental, beyond earth, beyond space, and outside of time. Since there is only *one substance*, there is no space; there is no time. Then there is no central source in a specific location, nor is there a source that has a specific origin or beginning outside of *the substance*. Location and origin imply a point of reference within space-time. In order to have location, you must have a reference point in space-time to say this location is separate from that location. Since there is *only one substance*, how could there be location? Location would imply two separate or individual substances. An origin not only implies a point in space-time from which things originate, but an origin also implies a beginning (in time) and an originator. Beginnings are in time, a place where things start, which implies time. Time exists in language only. *There is no beginning* because there is *only one substance*. Location implies space-time. Origin implies space-time. Source implies an originator, which somehow is separate from space-time, which sources or produces or creates something. How can this be when there is *only one substance*? There is no location, origin, or originator that exists outside of the words "location" and "origin" and "originator." Location, origin, and originator exist in language only. Space and time are metaphoric representations and they exist in language only.

CHAPTER 13

ARCHETYPES AND PROTOTYPES

"STRUCTURAL SEED STORY"
Recently, I had an experience with a Buddhist teacher who, during the workshop, evoked a deity in Buddhism; and you could feel the energy and power of that particular deity. What about these archetypes?

"A": Historically, structuralists (about 1900–1965) saw *types* within mythology. We see this tendency now in diagnosis: character structures and the enneagram. Archetypes, or prototypes, are the original or first or primary types that types come from. Carl Gustav Jung mistakenly taught that archetypes are universal. For Jung, they exist in this "other" world, which he called the collective unconscious, and he claimed that these archetypes rule our lives, rather than appreciating that these archetypes or myth-types are deeply rooted cultural beliefs that might even be passed down through the generations. These structures do organize the "I," but they have no separate individual existence or purpose.

Symbols are not universal, they are cultural. For example, in the Christian world, snakes are bad. In the Greek myths, heroes return as snakes after death to give information. In the West, from 1900 onward, dreams of sleeping with Mom (Oedipus Complex) is a myth that, for Jung and Freud, revealed a universal repressed wish. For the Greeks, on the other hand, dreams of sleeping with Mom could mean good fortune.

Secondly, and more importantly, like Plato's prototypes that exist in "another world," archetypes exist in language only. Myths have functions in primitive society as early indigenous science; or to support cultural regulations or rituals, which announce different stages or jumps in biological development; and/or to mediate contradictions. <u>Archetypes and mythologies are structural *seed* stories passed down from generation to generation and, as such, they have power</u>.

In quantum psychology, archetypes can be viewed as condensations of the forces and dimensions of the quantum world, i.e., energy, space, mass, time, gravity, light, electromagnetics, light, sound, dark matter, etc. Prior to the archetype, and prior to the physics dimensions from which archetypes are made, is **NOTHING-NESS,** or *the substance.* Each archetype, because it is a condensation of the physics dimension, has a certain intrinsic "power." By evoking a deity through mantra, evoking a deity through yantra, or evoking a deity through tantra, you are evoking the "power" of that particular condensation of the physics dimensions, which forms the archetype.

The problem is the illusion of an archetype (seed story ritual, early indigenous science, etc.) that will lead to a utopian *"Nirvana."* Ultimately, acting-out the archetypal structure, or practicing an archetypal ritual or organizing belief leads to entrapment because it presupposes the "reality" of the archetype (seed story) and the "you" that is aware of the archetype, "as if" they are made of separate substances. There is *no* "you," and there is no archetype. "Prior" to both of them is *the substance.* Much of spiritual practice is archetypal/ mythological, and by declaring "doership" of a traditional "spiritual practice," you will reinforce the "you" that imagines it does the practice (the "archetypal ritual-spiritual" seed story) and the "you" with the mythology, which imagines that it will "get salvation" or a utopian Nirvana by performing the archetype/myth-type ritual. It's very circular; and it is a game.

Simply put, so-called "spiritual paths" are archetype/myth-types, and *you cannot get out of an archetypal/mythological/psychological (seed story) from inside the archetype/myth-type/psych-type (seed story), nor by acting out the archetype/myth-type/psych-type.* Rather, you continue to bring about the power and the energy of the condensation, and "you" might feel more powerful, but never free of it. There is no way out of an archetype/myth-type seed story (*spiritual path*) or any *language game* that is deeply held and passed down from generation to generation. The only way out of an archetype/myth-type is to "see" through it. *You cannot get out of an archetype/myth-type by practicing the archetype myth-type or by acting out the archetype/myth-type from inside archetypal or mythological rituals.*

"STRUCTURAL SEED STORY"
*Carl Gustav Jung said that each of us has masculine
and feminine archetypes that need to be integrated.*

"A": Jung's mistake was in imagining that the concepts of masculine, feminine, and all the other archetypes and/or myth-types (seed stories, *language games*) have a purpose and need to be integrated into our psyches. Jung, like us all, was a product of his discursive structure. In Jung's formative years, Plato was still in vogue; hence, archetypes (prototypes) "rule" us, or determine us and our behavior. Structuralism (1940s) and postmodernism (1966 to present) broke down structural seed stories as yet another logo-centered structure. Jung, being a product of his discourse, went along for the pre-structural ride. Jung was not aware of Levi-Strauss' de-centering; therefore, Jung posited that the new structure or archetypes have a life in this "other world" (the collective unconscious), instead of Plato's land of forms or perfected ideas, which we must now integrate. The concept of a collective unconscious or other world can be viewed as an archetype myth-type too, which should be deconstructed and not integrated, as some existent thing.

It was unfortunate that Jung did not live long enough to see his Archetypal structures collapse in structuralism or in Derrida's deconstruction, and also in the work of Ludwig Wittgenstein who demonstrated that all existence, or structure, or an "I," exists in, and is only part of, a *language game*.

You must understand that to find out *who you are*, you have to find out who *you are not*, and you are not your archetypes (seed stories), so why would you want to integrate a myth-type/archetype when who you are, or *the substance*, is prior to the archetypes? Therefore, to find out who you are, you must deconstruct the archetypal seed stories!!!

Archetypes have power. Apples have tastes, anger has blood rushing through you, but what does power, energy, archetypes or integrating some psyche have to do with discovering who you are?

The second thing that must be clear about archetypal seed stories is that the concept of archetypes requires existence, an "I" to say "That is an archetype." The "*I am*" is an archetype, and all the naming of the archetypes arises neurologically from the "food body" after the events and actions have already taken place. Even the discerning of a pattern is the nervous system suggesting or seeing a pattern so the nervous system can learn the pattern, and won't repeat that pattern, enabling it to survive better. It's a neurological process. The nervous system, in order to survive, wants to understand and learn about the pattern so it doesn't repeat the pattern, or so it can choose another pattern. The awar<u>er</u> (or the one that becomes aware of, or notices, a particular pattern) is also an abstraction of the nervous system, and this awar<u>er</u> arises after the actions and events have already taken place. Therefore, there really are no patterns. There are only observ<u>ers</u> or awar<u>ers</u> or "I"'s that become aware of patterns and label them as patterns. In this way, structures and patterns are abstractions. There are no patterns, only *one substance* and *there is no "what is."* Hence, in Suzuki Roshi's book, *Zen Mind, Beginner's Mind,* with the beginner's mind, there are no patterns. There is no "I" that formulates patterns. Therefore, every "moment" is a "new moment." It is not a moment that is "viewed" as a pattern or representation. The "realization" occurs when the "food body" stops producing an "I."

***WHEN WE SAY THEY ARE
ABSTRACTIONS OF WHAT IS,
WE MUST REALIZE
THERE IS NO WHAT IS.***

"A"

EASTERN PHILOSOPHY

CHAPTER 14

GURU AND DISCIPLE— TEACHER AND STUDENT

QUESTION
The guru knows who they are?

"A": Yes, however a guru cannot always teach how to "get" who you are. But there is no "are" that you are.

QUESTION
Does the guru teach by example?

"A": No!!! This is a major mistake. The body of the guru or teacher is *not* a model or example. To illustrate, "I" once spent time with a beautiful teacher, a guru named Baba Prakashananda. He was the most humble, loving, sweet person "I" have ever met. However, even these great qualities are still qualities of personality. Many people make the mistake of taking the guru's personality as significant. Hence, they imagine that what his/her personality does is more spiritual or has more meaning than it does. Don't fall in love with the guru's personality. *That one substance* is beyond at-

tribution. It is a great error to imagine that being more loving and compassionate are somehow "spiritual" qualities; they are still qualities of personality. Personality is a *language game*. Trying to create, have, possess, or act as if you "are" or "have" those personality traits is a "spiritual trap." Moreover, these qualities are binary. Love/hate, soul/body, compassion/passion; these imply that the former (love, soul, compassion) along with the person who possesses these gualities is pure and closer to a centralized origin or source than the latter (hate, body or passion) which has "fallen." There is only *one substance*, so how can anything be closer or farther away from it.

"*R*": Nisargadatta Maharaj once said this to "me": "Even the physical body of the guru is subject to the play of the gunas ('energies')."

QUESTION
Many gurus yell and seem to be of bad temperament. How can they help me?

"*A*": This is like the Ramana Maharishi story, in which he says, "If your house is on fire, why would you care what the color of the fireman's hair or clothes are?"

Don't worry about the personality or imagine that the personality means something; rather ask "yourself" and answer honestly; "After years of 'spiritual' practice, is there really a change, or am 'I' still miserable and depressed?" If you are miserable and depressed, (more or less) you've got the wrong spiritual teacher, guru, or path.

QUESTION
Isn't mantra a sound that signifies the source or origin?

"*A*": Mantra is an arbitrary sound. Its repetition brings about *reflection*, concentration, and relaxation. However, the key to mantra is to understand that the mantra, the deity of the mantra (what it signifies), and the repeater of the mantra, are one. The mantra is a tool used to develop concentration which is step six which leads to step seven, meditation in most yogas.

To understand that, the sound of the mantra, the deity, not the words, but the sound, and the repeater of the mantra (the sound, not the word "I"), are all made of sound and are *the same substance*. The differences are linguistic and exist in language only. The mantra *stands in* for the deity, but the mantra has no meaning outside of language. There are no pre-existing deities outside of language. The deity is also an abstraction of **NOTHING**; the word "deity" denotes a concept with a meaning that is "always already" deferred and abstracted. For example, if I say, "What is the meaning of love?" You say, "Love is a feeling in the heart. "I" say, "What's a feeling?" "You" say, "A sensation." "I" say, "What's a sensation?" "You" say, "Energy moving through my body that makes me feel more alive." "I" ask, "What's life?" So each concept *defers* to another concept; therefore, it can have no meaning in itself. Wittgenstein said, "The meaning of words is in their use," but there is no pre-existing meaning, or as Saussure said, "*There are no ready-made ideas that exist outside of language.*" When the "I" inquires, "What is 'I'?" everything disappears.

"*A*": (On a Roll):

I

By the mere naming of an object, we imagine it has existence. It is as if by giving an object a name, we say it *is*. We assume that "it" or "I" must exist because it has a name. We then analyze why or how it exists, not to mention its origins, and reasons. Soon schools are formed to defend, attack, or analyze the existence of the named object or "I." Things exist in name only, they are abstractions of **NOTHING**. In fact, there is no reality outside of the word "reality," which is a word that *stands in* for other words whose meanings are always deferred to other words, which just name things.

II

Religion imagines a soul separate from the body. The soul is conceived to be higher than the body. The body is lower, hence all materializing and naturalizing from anger to love, from reproduction to eating, is deemed lower than the soul, and is something to be overcome.

All urges are natural and they occur in the "old brain" (hypothalamus). The "new brain" (cortex), through language and socialization, labels many of our natural impulses as bad, and imagines a soul, which is good. In this way, the soul/God concept is used to destroy or kill the real spirit or the natural life force of the body.

III

The archetype (mythology) of a soul going to Heaven or to the land of perfect forms has been a nightmare for humans who imagine that they are sinners, but it has been a great business for religion.

IV

All is abstracted perception and language; and since there is only a self or "I," as long as there is a language that yields a perceiver, then what we call "I" is a combination of phenomena or impressions that come out of the food body.

The chemicals of the nervous system fabricate the self and "I" as a metaphor, and produce perceptions that make the world appear as solid, unchanging, and persisting. When we look at someone, we perceive a body that, through the habit of the consciousness of association, brings forth the concept of their perceived identity. It is an attribute of consciousness that connects the gap or space between perceptions, making them appear changeless, constant, and permanent. All identity, all sense of "I," is an abstraction, a linguistic appearance; it is elusive at best, and an illusion at worst. Because all is *constant movement* of "energy" at one level, and a representation at another, there is no constant, unchanging "self" or "I." Rather, the self or "I" appears and disappears. It is like an electron whose existence is inferred; it exists only when it is reflected upon. It is reflection that creates the concept of a self or "I."

V

Rationalism and religion imagine a primary cause, which they label as a centralized figure called "God" who exists in a specific location. Assigning causation is a habit of the nervous system, a habitual "mental" process. Within this designation of a primary-cause centralized figure called "God" lies two false assumptions: 1) there is more than one substance; and 2) the "I" can do something about it. It is in the latter where the bind lies. The "I," a linguistic concept and abstraction of the nervous system, which arises after the action has occurred, claims doership and ownership of thoughts and actions, and claims doership of the spiritual, moral, or psychological actions, rather than understanding that its doership and perceivership arises after the fact and is still only *the substance.*

VI

For Confucius, he is not an originator, he is a transmitter, part of the ripple in the wave, always in process. Unlike in the West, we imagine originators. In the West, origination is good, rather than carrying along a tradition.

For postmodernism, everything is already in the text, or language. Speech is just a suppression or marginalization of one text over another, there is no originator, or original.

VII

IS

The word and representation *is* makes the representation appear to exist, "as if" the word *is* was not a representation, but that existence actually is, or does exists. The word *is* represents a sound that gives the "illusion of being" manifestation and existence in time when, actually, it serves only as a linguistic tool to define and represent the space-time name of the representation of existence. This representation of *is* makes us imagine that it is a *real* thing, which exists, gives the illusion of presence and essence. The linguistic word and abstraction *is* represents presence and essence, and bestows on a person the illusion of existence, which is just a linguistic word representation. The words *existence* and *is* are linguistic abstract representations.

VIII

Each perception and thought or idea was once a sensation and was once sensed, and later became an impression. There is no "mind" according to Wittgenstein, it is merely a metaphor for some "part" of the nervous system, which puts things together and constructs ideas. David Hume wanted to investigate ideas to see whether they were constructed in a way that does not correspond to reality. Hume asked, From which impression does this idea originate? He wanted, first of all, to determine which individual ideas went into the making of complex ideas. This would provide him with a critical method by which to analyze our ideas. Our structural seed stories ranging from God to Heaven and Hell, to liberation and sin and virtue is a cluster of many smaller ideas. For example, God lives in the sky; God created the universe; God watches us and wants the best for us. All of these are complex ideas in themselves. According to Hume, our idea of God consists of many simple smaller single ideas, such as "up there," all good, white-robed guy with a white beard. Hume suggested that we (the nervous system) had cut and pasted all these simple impressions into one big idea. He emphasized that all of the parts, which we associated with each other and fused together, were at some point in time entered into the nervous system as a simple impression. Hume believed that all thoughts and ideas could be traced back to corresponding *sense perceptions* and *sensation*.

In life, we use complex ideas without stopping to ask, "Are these ideas valid?" For example, regarding the question of "I" or the ego, for the word "ego," the question would be, "What is ego as a complex idea?" The *mistaken notion* of having a *constant* unalterable ego is a false perception, an abstraction (although all perception is false because it is an abstraction). The perception of ego is a long chain of simple impressions that have been fused together. The perception of "I" is a collection of different sensations (sense impressions), which fuse with each other. David Hume insisted that we have no underlying personal identity beneath or behind these sensations and sense perceptions, which come and go. Nisargadatta Maharaj said they were like pictures in a film-strip that move so rapidly that we do not register the spaces between the pictures, nor their lack of connection. Simply put, the pictures are not connected. The film is a collection of images fused together. Both David Hume, Nisargadatta Maharaj, and the Buddha saw life as a succession of mental and physical processes, which give people (the nervous system) the concept of change. Everything exchanges into something else: Molecules and atoms are constantly in flux, exchange, and change. The "I" is in the same situation. Nothing "I" can say is "me," said Buddha; hence, the Buddhist doctrine that everything is impermanent.

There is no "I" or unchangeable ego (state). *It is not the individual who forms the language, it is the language that forms the individual!!*

"R": WOW.

"A": By the way, the Buddha in the *Diamond Sutra* was clear that there were no molecules or world, that these were abstracted representations of **NOTHING**, including the "I" or perceiv<u>er</u> that is aware of the **void** when this is "gotten," the **void voids** itself. This is **SUNYATA**.

SECTION V

EAST AND WEST—
WHAT IS WORTH SAVING?

CHAPTER 15

WHAT IS WORTH SAVING?

"STRUCTURAL SEED STORY"
What is the essence of Buddhism and Hinduism?

"A": The essence of Buddhism leads us to the question, What is it that needs to be and should be saved? What is worth saving in Hinduism is the *one substance* called *Advaita-Vedanta,* and the negating, **Neti-Neti,** of everything, including the perceiver. What needs to be saved; there is only *one substance,* call that substance *Brahma,* call that substance *God,* or *undifferentiated consciousness, emptiness,* etc. That is what must be held continually in the "understanding," along with the "I" arising after the action or event. Buddha also teaches that there is no self or "I." Everything is impermanent. Everything is made of the same substance as everything else.

In Buddhism there is no permanence; there is no self. There is no separate, individual self, which incarnates again and again and again. What's worth saving in Buddhism? It is the understanding that there is only the *Buddha nature,* call that *Buddha nature* Brahma, call that Buddha nature *consciousness,* call that Buddha nature *God,* call that Buddha nature **void.** You can call it whatever you want, you never can say what it *is*. You can only say what it *is not*.

In Nagarjuna's Madhyamika (Middle Way) Buddhism, you could say that substance is *thusness*. There is no independent origination; all things, which occur depend on everything else. There is no independent action. "You" are like a drop of water in the ocean; you don't know that you're part of the ocean. Everything is made of the same substance as everything else. Everything "causes everything else." Everything occurs because everything else is going along in the same direction. What else is worth saving? There is no independent cause and effect. There is only total interconnection, no separate independent origination or originator, no awareness of enlightenment, no dharmas or path, no world (*Diamond Sutra*). The Heart Sutra actually could be looked at in levels: 1) form *becomes* emptiness — emptiness *becomes* form; 2) form *is* emptiness, emptiness *is* form; and 3) *there is no form or emptiness.*

Summary
1. Form is emptiness, emptiness is form. (*Heart Sutra*)
2. There is no world. (*Diamond Sutra*)
3. There is no independent origination.
4. There is no permanence.
5. There is no separate, independent self or soul.

"STRUCTURAL SEED STORY"
Why does Buddhism seem to say that there is NOTHING?

"A": There is no self and **NOTHING**, because if everything is *that one substance*, if everything is the ocean, then there is no self to declare that everything is the ocean, then there is **NOTHING**, but not in the sense of a nothing as the opposite of something. Nirvana is not an "experience." *Nirvana means extinction* and *unawareness*. It is not awareness, it is not perceivable. It is *unawareness* because, as the Buddha himself has said, "You will not even be aware of your own enlightenment." Why? Because there is no 'I' that will know it." Or, as Baba Prakashananda said, "If you become liberated, you will not be there to appreciate it." The world is an appearance made of the *one substance*, which has come, and it will go; it has arisen, and it will subside. This is "understanding" that is worth saving.

But even more noteworthy, many a seeker reaches the **void;** however, when the "experienc<u>er</u>" or "knower, or "awar<u>er</u>" of the **void** is just an abstraction and the experience of **void** a representation—then both disappear; this is *Sunyata*, the **voiding** of **void**, or as Nisargadatta said, "You are the child of a barren woman."

Appreciate that most people say, "it's all an illusion," without understanding two things: First, the perceiv<u>er</u> of the illusion is part of the illusion; and second, an illusion is something that appears to *be* and to *exist*, but it does not. Again, this is *Sunyata*; this is the understanding that you are the child of a barren woman; there is no Nirvana; there is no Walden III.

"STRUCTURAL SEED STORY"
But what is really IT in Buddhism?

"A": The *Heart Sutra: Form is none other than emptiness, emptiness is none other than form.* The *Diamond Sutra: Forsake all Dharmas; there are no molecules or atoms or world. There is no independent origination; hence, no separate independent self-nature. Everything is impermanent. There is an appearance of a world and, in short, it is a mirage.*

These particular understandings are the only understandings that need to be held in order to be "free," or *beyond free* and *not free*. If you think that an "I" can do it, you are on a never-ending cycle of doing, not doing, doing, not doing, doing, not doing. Most paths, the Buddhist path and the Hindu path included, create standards of actions, standards of behavior, standards of emotional experience, all of which are just standards measurable by some context that, in the end, will only enslave. **There is no "experience" of enlightenment, because *Nirvana means extinction;* there is no separate, independent self; so what self could be doing a path or process? There is no self or soul or viewpoint that exists outside of language. There is no enlightenment outside the word "enlightenment." Enlightenment exists in language only.**

Enlightenment, like all experiences, is an abstraction because it requires an "I" or experiencer to experience or know it! There is no enlightenment outside of the word "enlightenment." There is no liberation or bondage outside of the words "liberation" or "bondage." This is what Nisargadatta Maharaj meant when he asked, "How can an entity (self), which is a fiction, become enlightened?" When he said that it is all a concept, he meant that it is all words that exists as a *language game*, in words only: there is no existence or nonexistence outside of the words "existence" or "nonexistence."

Beliefs carry with them the illusion
of presence or pre-sound existence
and a point of reference
or center from which this "self" operates.
When beliefs are deconstructed,
the illusion of a self, in a particular location
with a center, vanishes along with the
illusion of a pre-sound existence sometimes
referred to as presence. This leads to the
"blankness" (which is not) that is
prior to presence existence
and absence non existence.
There is no perceiver;
it too is an abstraction,
a representation of nothing;
the perceiver is NOT.

"A"

CHAPTER 16

WESTERN PHILOSOPHY

"STRUCTURAL SEED STORY AND QUESTION"
Heidegger asked, "What is 'being'?"

"*A*": The concept of *being* is a representation. There is no "being," just a representation of being. Heidegger asked the right question: What is being, and hence began to analyze what being is, and what are its elements or its composition. Heidegger wanted to integrate a being to see what it is, or what constitutes being. Heidegger unfortunately falls into the trap of analyzing "what is being" or "what is the meaning of being?" Hence, Heidegger loses his direction; it would have been better to realize that there is *no being* and to dismantle that concept of *being* along with all the constituents, which hold the *is of being* in place. Heidegger stops short by "moving forward" and believing that there is a being, which exists in time, rather than dismantling the concept of being at its core. In short, Heidegger tried to define a being, which is not.

"STRUCTURAL SEED STORY"
There is a central being.

"A": We must understand that intrinsic to all words is the belief that words represent things that actually exist. Words are abstractions, metaphors that are representions of **NOTHING**. Moreover, abstracted words give the illusion that somehow, to name something is to give it existence.

The word *is* is a metaphor, a word (sound and representation) that we assume actually *is*, rather than just a word (representation) that describes an abstraction called *existence*. The abstraction *is*, or *existence*, exists in language only. Prior to language, what is this *is* or *existence*?

As an aside, "I" could say that the "I" is produced by chemicals; but chemicals are made of smaller components, such as molecules, which are made of atoms, which are made of sub-atomic particles, which change and exchange as electrons move about. There is no permanent self, being, or state. Even the subatomic particles and the perceiver of them are abstractions of **NOTHING**.

"STRUCTURAL SEED STORY AND QUESTION"
We should reflect on "What is being?" (Heidegger).

"A": The "food body" creates self-consciousness and reflection and an "I" which reflects, to mediate and aid in its survival. All understanding is rooted in time. Since being is time related, and time and being are concepts (existing only in language), the understanding generated by being and time are just concepts of concepts, abstractions of abstractions which is a *language game*.

"STRUCTURAL SEED STORY"
Space and time is **a priori** *to any experience.*
(Immanuel Kant).

"A": Kant reflects on this notion in space-time; hence, he comes to a space-time conclusion. However, the experience and the experienc<u>er</u> arise with the perception of space-time; there is no space-time or experienc<u>er</u> without a perceiv<u>er</u> or awar<u>er</u>, or know<u>er</u>. Therefore, space-time is not *a priori* to experience, rather, space-time is part of the "I"'s experience. The "I" and space-time are inseparable. "Space" is a representation, and "time" exists in language only; hence, <u>Kant unknowingly played a speculative *language game*</u>, which included the representation of "space" and the language of "space-time."

In short, it can be said that Heidegger presupposed being. Heidegger analyzes being. We want to, as Nisargadatta Maharaj did, deconstruct being as a fiction.

Simply stated, what needs to be gotten from Heidegger's book, *Being in Time,* is the enquiry into the "being" concept and "time," not as a real development of some type of "how to" or what *is,* but as what *is not,* since being and time are both abstracted representations. Unfortunately Heidegger treated being as an *is,* which exists.

"STRUCTURAL SEED STORY AND QUESTION"
Where do being or the "I" sense come from?

"A": Nature.

"STRUCTURAL SEED STORY AND QUESTION"
Heidegger also inquired, "Why is there something rather than nothing?"

"A": The arising of being is like a wave in the ocean. It arises and subsides. When the neurons turn off, there is nothing. When the neurons turn on, there is something, some people call this *spanda*. Asking "Why?" always presupposes that there is a reason. Asking "Why?" is the wrong question because it presupposes an answer. Both why and the answer exist in abstracted language only and represent a *language game*.

BEING IS NOTHING.
NOTHING IS BEING.
SOMETHING IS NOTHING.
NOTHING IS SOMETHING.
THERE IS NO SUCH THING AS BEING OR NOTHING.

"STRUCTURAL SEED STORY"
There is an "is" and an existence.

"A": The word and representation *is* makes other representations appear to "be" and to "exist," as if the word *is* was not a representation for existence, but actually exists. The word (representation) describes *is*, a sound that gives the illusion of manifestation and beingness when, actually, it serves only to define and represent the space-time name of a representation. Hence the word (representation-name) *is* gives the illusion of presence and essence (which contains

a pre-supposition of prior real existence). Both terms represent a thing or a person giving it the illusion of existence and beingness, which is also just a word representation and symbol of an abstracted representation and a cultural sound.

There tends to be an assumption of being because the nervous system "wants" to reconcile the "I"'s "thrownness"; we assume a being to handle our thrownness. Simply stated, just as an "I" exists in language only, so too *is*, exists in language only.

"STRUCTURAL SEED STORY AND QUESTION"
How does the Buddhist perspective translate into daily life?

"A": A modern philosopher, Jacques Derrida, speaks in terms similar to those of Nagarjuna's Madhyamika Buddhism. Derrida uses the word "differance" ("diffe*r*ance" with an *"a"*) to demonstrate that for every word you use, you must use a second word to define it, and still another word to define the second word, and yet another word to define the third word, and another word to define the fourth word, and so on. In the end, you see that all language always *refers* to or is *deferred* to another word to describe it. This means that meaning is always deferred or postponed or, simply stated, you can never get back to meaning. The beauty of Jacques Derrida in relation to Madhyamika Buddhism is that you have a middle path, constant movement between good and bad, high and low, right and wrong, sin and virtue, and there is a *space in between*. The *space in between* is the space between different frames (like the space between two pictures in a film strip, as Nisar-

gadatta said), which is also called the space between two thoughts, or the space between two breaths. Derrida unfreezes words, hence they deconstruct. Nagarjuna deconstructs words and concepts until there is <u>no</u> <u>*thing*</u>.

"QUESTION"
Are there other Western philosophers who knew this?

"*A*": Yes. There are about four Western philosophers who are worth saving in this context. The beginning parts of Spinoza (which got him excommunicated from the Jewish religion): Spinoza's '*only one substance.*' Wittgenstein's 'anything you say is in language only, and is a *language game.*' Nietzsche's 'there is no truth with a capital T.' Jacques Derrida's 'free play or movement from one binary concept to the other.' These are indirectly part of Madhyamika (Middle Way) Buddhism, and they are worth saving.

CHAPTER 17

TAOISM
AND CHINESE THOUGHT

"QUESTION"

What is worth keeping in Taoism
and other Chinese thought?

"A": If we're talking about the realization of the underlying substance, *that one substance*, then we have to look at the story of Taoism in two different ways. First, everything is "chi" in Taoism. Everything is chi; and a chair, a table, a thought, an idea, a thing called a "person," is also made of condensed chi.

In Taoism, they use the *I-Ching or the Book of Changes*. What's important about this book is that it maps out 64 possible places (like snapshots) where you are in relationship to these changes. In other words, if I am in "my" life *here* at Point A, how do I get to Point B? "I am" in a state of change; where am "I" in relations to the changes? This is worth keeping.

What's not worth keeping, is the *I-Ching*'s divination process, or its underlying implicit belief that if "I" know where "I" am, a separate, individual, independent "I" can change it. Because change implies a separate, independent "I," which, first of all, is not (because there is only *one substance*); secondly, on a biological level, the "I" that perceives arises after the event, action, and experience has already taken place; and thirdly, an "I" that could do something would require an independent self nature and origination, which, according to Buddha, cannot be. There is only *"dependent arising,"* meaning that everything is one unit and "moves" as one unit. Even worse is the misconception and ultimate trap that "I" can also create *chi*, "I" should have more *chi*, "I" should develop *chi*. This might help your health and energy level, but it will not help you find out who you are. The question to consider is prior to the story of *chi*: Who are you?

Going with the flow is understanding that we are a droplet of water in the ocean, connected to everything else, which is made of the *same substance* as everything else, with no independent self nature, or independent origination. This is worth saving.

DECONSTRUCTING
THE APPROACH

How could *"A," "R,"* or an "I" for that matter, bring to an "end" a text that on its surface appears to both graft together different texts as well as deconstruct most of what Western, and even Eastern philosophy, religion, and psychology has posited and assumed to be true?

This, however is a surface position. After we uncover the language that binds, or the language that hopes to liberate, we embark upon *post-deconstruction.*

Before we conclude, as promised in the beginning of the text, to deconstruct our prongs of deconstruction, let us make sure that we understand language. Firstly, *there is no language of the spirit.* Hegel and others believed that this spirit wanted to incarnate. Still others believe that spirit speaks through us. Let me assure you that *the substance* doesn't *want* to speak or incarnate, because it does not have a nervous system. Secondly, even if *the substance* wished to speak and did speak through a person, more than 99% of it would be omitted in the process of abstracting and transducing sound into speech. Then, even if an "I" heard spirit speaking through someone, the words would be a simulation, an abstracted representation of **NOTHING.**

Words and maps are a reproduction of a reproduction, with no original, because if there is only *the one substance*, there can be no separate *thing*, and if "it" somehow spoke, it would have to go through a nervous system. But even more to the point, there is no spirit outside of the word "spirit"; it is all in language only, and the language of spirit, whatever people may say it says, is representational, an abstraction of **NOTHING**, and a *language game*.

FROM THE METOPHOR OF POSTMODERNISM AND LINGUISTICS TO POST-DECONSTRUCTION

In the beginning of the text, we were going to use postmodern deconstruction as one of our six-prong approaches to dismantling structural seed stories. But before we deconstruct postmodern deconstruction, let us first appreciate its similarities to Wittgenstein and his brilliance. Both of these point us in the direction of the major culprit of our problems: language, as does Advaita-Vedanta, the early Vedic Grammarians, and Madhyamika (Middle Way) Buddhism does.

Postmodern Deconstruction gets us to explore and "go beyond," not only the language of the "I," but it also refers to all its stories as narratives and meta-narratives[17]. However, unlike Advaita-Vedanta or Madhyamika (Middle Way) Buddhism, this leaves Postmodern Deconstruction as just another philosophical *language game*, unless we begin to deconstruct the metaphor of the deconstruction process.

---

[17] These are global world views that explain everything. Meta-narratives assume the validity of their own truth claims. In the work of Jean Francois Lyotard, a grand narrative is a universal explanatory theory that admits no opposition to its principles.

Postmodern deconstruction *unfreezes meaning*, rather than actually deconstructing it. For us, the three basic approaches of Postmodern Deconstruction follow:

1. It de-centers (see Figure A).
2. It denies dichotomies (called binaries).
3. It destroys hierarchy.

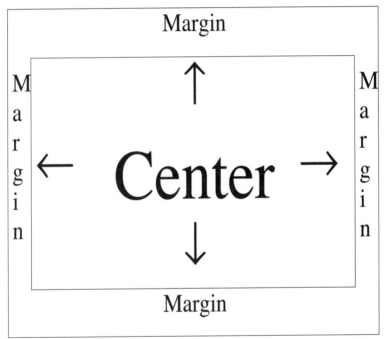

Figure A   Declaring a localized center pushes its opposite to the margins. De-centering is smashing a center and a margin.

We de-center, because once a center is established, it automatically moves its binary opposite to the margins (Figure A). Postmodernism *unfreezes* rather than freezes movement from the center to the margins; this is where the problem lies. To illustrate, let us imagine the dichotomy of love/hate. Someone might have hate in the center, love at the margins. We de-center by un-freezing the binary (which is linguistic), so in Derrida's words there is a "free-play" of love/hate, hate/love. The problem is that deconstruction now becomes a new hierarchy, and we still become trapped in the deconstruction game of deconstruction as a *language game*.

In this way, deconstruction has its own metaphysics or system of words and *language game*s, which can continue on forever, with the hope or dream of a utopian Nirvana or not Nirvana, continuously in the play of deconstruction, or unfreezing meaning.

This is how postmodern deconstruction becomes yet another *"free language game,"* which better promotes and promises some form of "freedom," yet leaves us in the world of a representational language which is an abstraction of **NOTHING**.

ADVAITA-VEDANTA

The one substance of Advaita, coupled with the **Neti-Neti,** (sanskrit for not this not that) of Vedanta, forms a powerful combination in deconstruction. It first breaks up everything because nothing is; *"as the one substance,"* not even "I."

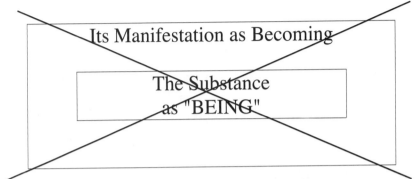

Figure B   Here the one substance destroys the binary belief that the substance is different from what it "becomes"; thus liberating us from a linguistic separate from the substance.

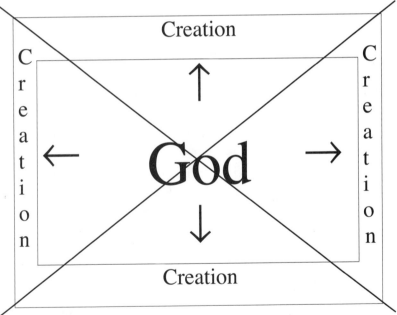

Figure C   This makes God the center of its creation. One substance de-centers and liberates us from the binary. In other words, GOD (The Substance) is no longer separate from its creation.

Deconstructing the Metaphor of the One Substance

However, there is actually not *one substance*; the realization of the *one substance* can occur only if an "I" (in some form, i.e., witness, awar<u>er</u>, perceiv<u>er</u>, etc.) is present. When the "I-perceiver" dissolves, we are left with *YOU ARE NOT* as a linguistic metaphoric way of saying the last thing that could be said, the last *not this*. Although Advaita often calls Brahman the *one substance*. There is no substance or *one substance* without an abstracted "I" to say it is so.

Deconstructing the Metaphor of the Neurological Understanding

The neurological understanding has been used to demonstrate that the "I" arises after the event and action have already occurred. *The "I" fabricated by the nervous system is a metaphor.* This gives us the neuroscientific "understanding" of a basic tenet of yoga: "YOU ARE NOT THE DOER."

But, does the nervous system exist? The "I" that is fabricated by the nervous system and "thrown into the world" is an abstraction. The "I"-perceiv<u>ers</u>' view of a nervous system is also an abstraction of the abstracted "I," a representation of **NOTHING**; <u>the nervous system is a perception, a metaphor!!!</u> There is no world (*Diamond Sutra*), even the world is an abstraction. In Yoga, *Dristi Shristi Vada* comes from the Sanskrit, "There is no world without an 'I' there to perceive it." Since the "I"-perceiv<u>er</u> is a representation, an abstraction, what the "I" represents and perceives is an abstraction of an abstraction, a metaphor. Therefore, the nervous system and brain can be only an assumption, an inference, a metaphor, a possible guess, which, by the "I"'s own estimate, perceives less than 1% of the "incoming stimuli." Therefore, what the "I" perceives is not even close to an imagined *is*, as both are abstractions, representations of **NOTHING**. Does this nervous system abstracting, this representational apparatus, even exist? Like the world (*Diamond Sutra*), it exists only to the abstracted "I"-perceiver, which as an abstration is not.

Buddhism

Buddhism, specifically the *Heart Sutra*, "Form is none other than emptiness, emptiness is none other than form," and the *Diamond Sutra*, "There is no world"; all Dharmas should be forsaken," leads us further into the non-existence of the utopian Nirvana understanding of Walden III. Moreover, the nonpermanence and "no independent origination" and *dependent arising* leads us further into the **NOTHINGNESS**, "beyond" **NOTHINGNESS** (called *Sunyata*), and toward Nirvana as extinction. In Madhyamika Buddhism, Nagarjuna knows that behind or beyond this deconstruction is Nirvana. It should be noted and emphasized that *there is no Nirvana*. Nagarjuna deconstructs the *ism* in Buddh*ism* when he states, "*there is no Buddha who ever gave a teaching*," and since Nirvana is extinction, there is no Nirvana, no Buddha, and no Walden III.

It could be stated quite simply this way:

**THE SEER AND SEEN IS THE SAME.
THERE IS NO SEER AND SEEN.**

**FORM BECOMES EMPTINESS,
EMPTINESS BECOMES FORM.
FORM IS EMPTINESS,
EMPTINESS IS FORM.
THERE IS NO FORM OR EMPTINESS.**

THERE IS NO BUDDHA.
THERE IS NO NIRVANA.
THERE IS NO WALDEN III.

In this way, Buddhism ultimately deconstructs itself, leaving only a trace of hope, which Nagarjunas' Madhyamika Buddhism deconstructs.

DECONSTRUCTING THE METAPHOR OF QUANTUM PHYSICS

Quantum physics demonstrates and indirectly deconstructs all grand narratives by virtue of the fact that events are *probable* at best, and that they are chaotic. It is only an abstracted "self," which organizes and fabricates a physics that actually exists outside of the nervous system.

But probably the most striking of all is that matter and energy, space and time, which are our building blocks of any "theory of everything," are metaphors. Space-time and energy-matter are representations, perceptions and as such are metaphors, and they derive no meanings outside of the nervous system and language, whose existence in the former, and accuracy in the latter, can be deconstructed as names or descriptions of things, events, and interactions, which occur through the eyes of a perceiver. In short, Ludwig Wittgenstein said, "People take descriptions and make them rules." In this case, abstracted descriptions are metaphors made into laws of physics. Prior to language, or an abstracted perceiver; do space, mass, and time, even exist?

POST-DECONSTRUCTION

If we are now "beyond" the deconstruction process and grand narratives, where does that leave us? If everything is *the substance*, then there is no substance, no center, no originator or origin.

Nagarjuna's Madhyamika (Middle Way) Buddhism, along with Advaita-Vedanta, de-constructs deconstruction itself, or **Neti-Netis** the **Neti-Neti** itself. For when the Madhyamika Buddhists have been accused of either positing another center or nihilism (the teaching that nothing exists), they reply, *"When a thing is not found, how can there be no thing?"* or *"I do not negate anything, nor is there anything to negate."*

The question arises then, using the Buddhist *Heart Sutra*, "Form is emptiness, emptiness is form," is there something?

Another way to say this is something is nothing, and nothing is something. However, most people imagine that the nothing actually *is* something. Both nothing and something are abstractions of **NOTH-ING** and exist in language only. There is no nothing or something. Or, when the **NOTHING** and its **perceiver** are both abstracted representations, then both dissolve. Then there is Nirvana as extinction and Walden III, which IS NOT.

"R": "I" asked Nisargadatta Maharaj a question. He replied,

> "There is no birth.
> There is no death.
> There is no person.
> It's all a concept, it's
> all an illusion!!!
> So now you know the **NOTHING**,
> and so now you can leave."

When I "got" (forgive the language) the definition of illusion, "*something that appears to exist, but does not exist,*" then "'I' realized" this: How could a person who appears to *be,* but *is not,* know, experience, or have Nirvana or Walden III?

Maybe that's the long and short of it.

With Love
Your Brother *"A"—"R"—"Stephen"*

GLOSSARY

The glossary was put together from several sources, with my own additions. Those sources appear below:

Audi, R., (Ed.). *The Cambridge dictionary of philosophy.* (1995, 1999). Cambridge, England: Cambridge University Press.

Glock, H.J. (1996). *Wittgenstein dictionary* (pp. 193-196). Malden, MA: Blackwelle.

Korzybski, A. (1993). *Science and sanity: An introduction to non-aristotelian systems and general semantics* (5th ed.). Brooklyn, NY: Institute of General Semantics.

Macy, D. (2000). *The Cambridge dictionary of critical theory.* London, England: Penguin Books.

Markos, L. (1999). *From Plato to postmodernism: Glossary and bibliography.* Chantilly, VA: The Teaching Company.

TERMS

Abstraction—In the context of this *Walden III* book, my use of the term "abstraction" refers to the work of Alfred Korzybski, who wrote, "We are immersed in a world full of "energy" manifestations, out of which we abstract directly only a very small portion, these abstractions being already colored by the specific functioning and structure of the nervous system—the abstractors." (Korzybski, *Science and Sanity*, p. 238) In explaining the process of abstracting, Korzybski wrote, "On the neurological level, what the nervous system *does* is abstracting . . . . The standard meaning of 'abstract' . . . implies 'selecting,' 'picking out,' 'separating,' 'summarizing,' 'deducting,' 'removing,' 'omitting,' . . . . We see that the term 'abstracting' implies structurally and semantically the activities characteristic of the nervous system, and so serves as an excellent *functional physiological* term." (Korzybski, *Science and Sanity*, p. 379). In the process of abstracting, the sense organs and nervous system are omitting billions of stimuli and selecting out only a fraction, less than 1%. This enables the nervous system to perceive and construct, out of "energy" in motion, an "I"/perceiver. This process of omitting or leaving out, which is performed by the nervous system, is called abstracting; and it is through this process that the "I" is created. An abstraction is a nervous system's "construction." The "I," the perceiver, and the perceived are metaphors constructed by the nervous system. The result of the abstracting process is called an abstraction; in this case, one abstraction is the "I" (subject) (the perceiver), and other abstractions are the physical world as well as the perceiver's emotional and ideological realities, all of these constructed out of **NOTHING.**

Binary—A set of two terms, in which one term is privileged over the other and considered better, closer to the logos (God, source) than the other; for example, being/becoming (being is closer to the logos than becoming), soul/body, emptiness/form, etc. When this is extended to "spirituality", then the person who possesses the first term as a quality is considered closer to God or the logos than one who does not possess the first quality, i.e., love/hate, virtue/sin, compassion/passion, etc.

Deep Structure—In structuralist theory, people are held to have deep structures or psychic systems that dictate how they operate. Underlying structures are the rules of internal as well as external dialogue.

Differance (differance with an *a*)—Pertaining to a process coined by Derrida, whereby meaning changes over time, and ultimately meaning is put off, postponed, or deferred forever. Coined by Derrida, the word functions most importantly on the word *defer*. Meanings are "always already" deferred as they always refer to other words. Thus meaning is never reached. This leaves one in an *aporia* (Greek for wayless)—in limbo and feeling anxious, because meaning can never be reached in language but is "always already" deferred (to other words, which defer to other words). The reference to "*differance*" takes up Saussure's argument that meaning is no more than the product of the differences between signs (words), coupled with a deferral system, meaning that language provides no stable meaning. Moreover there is no correspondence between signifier (sound) and signified (concept). In Saussure's language, all words are arbitrary. This is central to deconstructing the metaphysical tradition of the logos as the primal word.

Discourse—All that is written or spoken and all that invites dialogue and conversation. Same as *Langue* (Saussaure), discourse and *langue* both ventriloquize us, because it is prior to the arising of words thought, and the "I." The discourse tells us what we imagine we think, when actually the thought and the "I" is produced from the discourse before we realize it. Discourse is *not* a product of subjectivity of the "I," rather it produces the subjective "I's" metaphoric experience, which gets translated as narrative. In this way it has a constituent role in the production of symbolic systems that govern human existence.

Discursive Structures (Foucault)—Discursive structures are the products of discourses. It determines the role of the subject. Discourses refer to knowledge about objects. They do not have authors and are constituted by an anonymous collection of texts or language. In this way the discursive structure determines what we think; the discursive discourse ventriloquizes us: *we* are echoes of the *discourse*, not the other way around.

Language Game (Wittgenstein)—A way of using signs (words). What words mean is determined by how they are used. Wittgenstein said that usage determines meaning, and there is not a pre-existing mental image, or presence, or essence prior to language.

Language games (sentence, propositions or truth claims) are tautologies. Lyotard, borrowing Wittgenstein's language games, says that they contain their own rules, and conventions. A *language game* is a system of communication; it is linguistic activity guided by rules. A sentence is a "move" in the game of language; words and sentences are meaningless without the system or structure of which it is a part.

Philosophy confuses *language games*, that is, using the words of one language game according to the rules of another language game. Each language game is autonomous (Glock, *Wittgenstein Dictionary*, pp. 193-196).

Therefore, language games are what metaphysics is made of, since the "I" and the metaphysics exist in language only, and there is no "I" or metaphysics outside of language.

Langue—The overall system of signs (Saussure). The *langue* lies deeper than thought, and actually produces the language (speech) that makes thoughts, and hence words, possible. Similar to discourse or discursive structure, Foucault said "as thoughts are made of words; speech occurs through the suppression of language." There are no ready-made (preexisting) ideas that exist outside of language (Saussure).

Logocentric—An adjective used to describe systems of thought that claim legitimacy by reference to external, universally true propositions.

Logocentrism—A structural order that provides phenomena with an origin, or that explains their nature, which, according to Derrida, is characteristic of Western philosophy from Plato onward. The *logos* is the origin and site of truth. *Logocentrism* refers to meaning that emanates from some *logos* or *originary* source (like God) that is pure and undefiled, and existed prior to this world.

Logos—Refers to the ultimate or primal center or presence or transcendental self that existed prior to this world or from which this world came. This center (God) gives meaning and purpose to all things and serves as a comparative reference point against which truth (with a capital *T*) can be determined.

Meta-Narratives—Global world views that explain everything. Meta-narratives assume the validity of their own truth claims. In the work of Jean Francois Lyotard, a grand narrative is a universal explanatory theory that admits no opposition to its principles.

Postmodernism—Whereas modern theory seeks to invert binaries and set up new structures of thought, postmodernism deconstructs binaries, which tends to privilege one structure or center over another. Moreover, postmodernism deconstructs all logos, center, presence or originary sources.

Presence—A metaphysical logo-centric term, *presence* signifies a belief in a center or logos that contains within it a pure being that is self-contained and self-existent. Postmodern deconstruction rejects presence as a center, as does existentialism. The existentialist "existence precedes essence" is a rejection of presence. Buddhism also rejects presence as a center: "There is no separate, independent self nature," "no independent arising or origination."

Representation—This is the result of abstracting. The nervous system *represents* or reproduces through the abstracting process a "picture" or metaphor of what is. For example, if you look at a tree, your eye-brain system constructs a visual image that *represents* a tree, it is not the tree itself—the "map" is not the "territory." To put it another way, the result of your nervous system abstracting only a small amount of the billions of stimuli ("energies" of the atomic world)is a visual "map" of the tree in your brain. This visual image is an abstraction; it is the result of your eye-brain system trying to make "sense" out of the chaos of billions of energies impinging on and stimulating your eye-brain system. Therefore, your resulting "sensation" is what we call "tree." However, what you see is only a representation an abstraction; The tree itself is not in your brain, but your representation (your map) is in your brain. More importantly, the perceiver, and the "I" which perceives and draws conclusions are also abstracted representations, produced by the nervous system, through abstractions <u>which are made of **NOTHING**</u>. Hence, what you see is a *simulation* a copy of a copy, of a copy, which has no original, or originary presence or origin.

Simulacrum—A copy of a copy for which there is no original. For Jean Baudrillard, signs (words) represent no deeper or hidden meaning, they represent only themselves.

BIBLIOGRAPHY

* Indicates important to read.

American College Dictionary. (1963). New York: Random House.

Aranja, H. (1983). *Yoga philosophy of Patanjali.* Albany, NY: State University of New York Press.

Audi, R., (Ed.). *The Cambridge dictionary of philosophy.* (1995, 1999). Cambridge, England: Cambridge University Press.

Ayer, A. J. (1946). *Language, truth and logic.* Dover, England.

Bahirjit, B. B. (1963). *The Amritanubhava of Janadeva.* Bombay: Sirun Press.

*Balsekar, R. (1982). *Pointers from Nisargadatta Maharaj.* Durham, NC: Acorn Press.

Baudrillard, J. (1983). *Simulations* (Nicola Dufresre, Trans.). New York: Semio Text.

Bentov, I. (1977). *Stalking the wild pendulum.* Rochester, Vermont: Destiny Books.

Berman, D. (1998). *The world as will and representation* (abridged). Dover, Charles, England: Tuttle Press.

Bohm, D. (1951). *Quantum theory.* London: Constable.

———— (1980). *Wholeness and the implicit order.* London: Ark Paperbacks.

Bois, J. S. (1978). *The art of awareness: A textbook on general semantics and epistemics* (3rd ed.). Dubuque, IA: William C. Brown Company.

*Buddha. (1969). *Diamond sutra.* (A. F. Price & M.-L. Wong, trans.). Boulder, CO: Shambhala.

*Buddhist Text Translation Society. (1980). *The heart sutra and commentary.* San Francisco: Buddhist Text Translation Society.

The Cambridge guide to early Greek philosophy. (1981). Cambridge, England: Cambridge University Press.

Camus, A. (1955). *The myth of Sisyphus and other essays,* New York, NY: Alfred A. Knopf.

Cane, R. J. (2000). *Jean Baudrillard.* New York: Routledge.

*Capra, F. (1976). *The tao of physics*. New York: Bantam Books.

*Chisholm, F. P. (1945). *Introductory lectures on general semantics*. Brooklyn, NY: Institute of General Semantics.

Coward, H. (1990). *Derrida and Indian philosophy* (p. 61). Albany, NY: State University of New York.

Coward, H. G., & Kunjunmi Raja, K. (1990). *The philosophy of the Grammarians*. Princeton, NJ: Princeton University Press.

Dawkins, R. (1978). *The selfish genes*.

Davison, R. (1997). *Camus: The challenge of Dostoyevsky*, Devon, England: University of Exeter Press.

Dostoyevsky, F.   *The brothers Karamazov* (pp. 255-274). New York: Modern Library.

*Dunn, J. (Ed.). (1982). *Seeds of consciousness*. New York, NY: Grove Press.

*——— (1985). *Prior to consciousness*. Durham, NC: Acorn Press.

*——— (1994). *Consciousness and the absolute*. Durham, NC: Acorn Press.

Edinger, E. (1992). *Ego and the archetype: Individualization and the religious function of the archetype*. Boston, MA: Shambhala.

Edwards, P. (Ed.). (1967). *The encyclopedia of philosophy* (eight volumes). New York/London: Macmillan Publishing Co., and The Free Press, Colliere Macmillan Publishers.

Encyclopedia of eastern philosophy and religion. (1989). Boston, MA: Shambala Press.

*Genova, J. (1991). *Wittgenstein: A way of seeing*. New York: Routledge.

Gleick, J. (1987). *Chaos*. New York: Penguin Books.

Glock, H.-J. (1996). *Wittgenstein dictionary* (pp. 193-196). Malden, MA: Blackwelle.

*Godman, D. (1985). *The teaching of Ramana Maharishi*. London: Ankara.

Gregory, R. L. (1970). *The intelligent eye*. New York: McGraw-Hill.

Gregory, R. L. (1978). *Eye and brain: The psychology of seeing* (3rd ed.). New York: McGraw-Hill.

Hawking, S. (1988). *A brief history of time*. New York: Bantam Books.

Hayakawa, S. I. (1978). *Language in thought and action* (4th ed.). New York: Harcourt, Brace, Jovanovich.

Heidegger, M. (2000). *Introduction to metaphysics* (R. Polk & G. Fried, Eds.). New Haven-Cordon, CT: Yale University Press.

Heidegger, M. (2001). *A companion to Heidegger's Introduction to Metaphysics* (R. Polk & G. Fried, Eds.). New Haven-Cordon, CT: Yale University Press.

Hopkins, J. (1987). *Emptiness yoga: The Tibetan middle way.* Ithaca, NY: Snow Lion Press.

Hua, T. (1980). *Surangama sutra.* San Francisco: Buddhist Text Translation Society.

Hume, D. (1883). *An inquiry concerning human understanding.* Indianapolis, IN: Hackett.

Ichazo, O. (1993). *The fourteen pillars of perfect recognition.* New York: The Arica Institute.

Isherwood, C., & Prhnavarla, S. (1953). *How to know God: The yoga of Patanjali.* CA: New American Library.

*Iyer, R. (Ed.). (1983). *The diamond sutra.* New York: Concord Grove Press.

James, W. (1994). *Varieties of religious experience.* New York: Modern Library.

Janssen, G. E. (Ed.). (1962). *Selections from science and sanity.* Brooklyn, NY: Institute of General Semantics.

Jnaneshwar. (1969). *Jnaneshwari, a song-sermon on the Bhagavad Gita.* Bombay, India: Blackie & Sons Publishers.

Kaku, M. (1987). *Beyond Einstein: The cosmic quest for the theory of the universe.* New York: Bantam.

———— (1994). *Hyperspace.* New York: Anchor-Doubleday.

Kaufmann, W. (1954). *The portable Nietzsche.* New York: Penguin Books.

King, M. A. (2001). *Guide to Heidegger's Being and Time.* (J. Llewelyn, Ed.). Albany, NY: State University of New York.

Korzybski, A. (1947). *Historical note on the structural differential* (audiotape). Brooklyn, NY: Institute of General Semantics. The text of this audiotape appears in *Alfred Korzybski: Collected Writings: 1920-1950* (M. Kendig, Ed.). Brooklyn, NY: Institute of General Semantics, 1990.

———— (1993). *Science and sanity: An introduction to non-aristotelian systems and general semantics* (5th ed.). Brooklyn, NY: Institute of General Semantics.

Krishnamurti, U. G. (1984). *The mystique of enlightenment: The unrational ideas of a man called U.G.* New York: Coleman.

———— (1988). *The mind is myth: Disquieting conversations with the man called U.G.* India: Dinesh Publications.

———— (1997). *The courage to stand alone.* New York: Plover Press.

Levi-Strauss, C. (1974). *Structural anthropology* (C. Jackson, Trans.). New York: Penguin Books.

Long, A. A. (Ed.). (1999). *The Cambridge companion to early Greek philosophy.* Cambridge, England: Cambridge University Press.

Lopez, Jr., D. S. (1988). *The heart sutra explained.* Albany, NY: State University of New York Press.

*Lyotard, J. F. (1982). *The postmodern condition.* Minneapolis, MN: University of Minnesota.

Macy, D. (2000). *The Cambridge dictionary of critical theory.* London, England: Penguin Books.

Markos, L. (1999). *From Plato to postmodernism: Glossary and bibliography.* Chantilly, VA: The Teaching Company.

Marx, K. (1872). *The essential writings.* New York: F. Bender.

McHoul, A., & Grace, W. (1993).   *A Foucault primer: Discourse, power, and the subject.* New York: New York University Press.

Mishra, R. S. (1968). *The textbook of yoga psychology of Patanjali's yoga sutras in all modern psychological disciplines.* New York: Julian Press/Crown Press.

Monk, R. (1990). *Ludwig Wittgenstein: The duty of genius* (J. Cape, Ed.). London: Penguin.

Mookerjit, A. (1971). *Tantra asana. A way to self-realization.* Basel, Switzerland: Ravi Kumar.

Mueller, C. G. (1965). *Sensory psychology.* Englewood Cliffs, NJ: Prentice-Hall, Inc.

Mulhall, S. (1996). *Routledge philosophy guidebook to Heidegger's Being and Time.* New York: Routledge.

Natoli, J. (1997). *A primer to postmodernity,* Malden, MA: Blackwelle.

Nietzsche, F. (1967). *Will to Power* (W. Kaufmann & R.J. Hollinsdale, Trans.). New York: Vintage Books.

Nietzsche, F. (1968). *Basic writing of Nietzsche.* (W. Kaufmann & R. J. Hollinsdale, Trans.). New York: Modern Library.

*Nisargadatta M. (1973). *I am that.* Durham, NC: Acorn Press.

Orage, A. R. (1974). *On love.* New York: Samuel Weiser.

*Osborne, A. (1960). *The collected works of Ramana Maharishi,* York Beach, ME: Samuel Weiser.

Ouspensky, P. D. (1949). *In search of the miraculous.* New York: Harcourt, Brace and World.

Plato. (1937). *The Dialogues of Plato* (B. Jowett, Trans.). New York: Random House.

Plato. (1937). *The Republic in Dialogues of Plato* (B. Jowett, Trans.). New York: Random House.

Poona, S. I. (1969). *Bhartrhari.* Poona, India: Deccan College.

*Powell, R. (Ed.). (1987) *The nectar of the Lord's feet.* England: Element Books. (Published in 1997 as *The nectar of immortality.* San Diego, CA: Blue Dove Press.)

*——— (1994). *The ultimate medicine.* San Diego, CA: Blue Dove Press.

*——— (1996). *The experience of nothingness.* San Diego, CA: Blue Dove Press.

*Pula, R. P. (1979). *General semantics seminar.* San Diego, CA: Educational Cassettes. (Album IV-D: set of six audiotapes distributed by the Institute of General Semantics).

Ree, J., & Chamberlain, J. (Eds.). (1998). *Kierkegaard: A critical reader.* Oxford, England: Blackwell.

Rosenau, P. M. (1992). *Postmodernism and the social sciences.* Princeton, NJ: Princeton University Press.

Russell, B. (1961). *The basic writings of Bertrand Russell.* New York: Simon & Schuster.

de Saussure, Ferdinand. (1966). *The course in general linguistics* (W. Baskin, Trans.). New York.

*Sawin, G. (2002–2003). The structural differential diagram. In *Et cetera: A Review of General Semantics, 59*(4) (Winter 2002); *60*(1) (Spring 2003); *60*(2) (Summer 2003); and *60*(3) (Fall 2003). Concord, CA: International Society for General Semantics.

Schulte, J. (1992). *Wittgenstein: An introduction.* State University of New York Press.

Shah, I. (1978). *Learning how to learn: Psychology and spirituality in the Sufi way.* San Francisco: Harper & Row.

*Singh, J. (1963). *Pratyabhijnahrdayam: The secret of self recognition.* Delhi, India: Motilal Banarsidass.

*——— (1979). *Siva sutra: The yoga of supreme identity.* Delhi, India: Motilal Banarsidass.

*——— (1979). *Vijnanabhairava: Divine consciousness.* Delhi, India: Motilal Banarsidass.

*——— (1980). *Spanda karikas: Lessons in the divine pulsation.* Delhi, India: Motilal Banarsidass.

Spinoza, B. (1957). *The ethics of Spinoza.* New York: Citadel Press.

*Spinoza, B. (1994). *The Ethics and other works.* Princeton, NJ: Princeton University Press.

Sprintzen, D. (1988). *Camus: A critical examination.* Philadelphia: Temple University Press.

Staten, H. (1982). *Wittgenstein and Derrida.* Oxford, England: Blackwell.

Suzuki, S. (1970). *Zen mind, beginner's mind.* New York: Weatherhill.

*Taimini, I. K. (1961). *The science of yoga.* Wheaton, IL: Theosophical Publishing House.

Talbot, M. (1987). *Beyond the quantum.* New York: Bantam Books.

Venkatesananda, S. (1976). *The supreme yoga.* Melbourne, Australia: Chiltern Yoga Trust.

*Weinberg, H. L. (1959). *Levels of knowing and existence: Studies in general semantics.* Brooklyn, NY: Institute of General Semantics.

Weiss, T. M., Moran, E. V., & Cottle, E. (1975). *Education for adaptation and survival.* San Francisco: International Society for General Semantics.

Wittgenstein, L. (1969). *On certainty.* Oxford, England: Blackwell.

*Wittgenstein, L. (1958). *Philosophical investigations.* Oxford, England: Blackwell.

*Wittgenstein, L. (1958). *The blue and brown books.* New York: Harper & Row, New York.

Wolinsky, S. H. (1991). *Trances people live: Healing approaches to quantum psychology.* Norfolk, CT: Bramble Co.

*——— (1993). *Quantum consciousness.* Norfolk, CT: Bramble Books.

——— (1993). *The dark side of the inner child.* Norfolk, CT: Bramble Co.

——— (1994). *The tao of chaos: Quantum consciousness* (Vol. II). Norfolk, CT: Bramble Books.

——— (1995). *Hearts on fire: The tao of meditation.* Capitola, CA: Quantum Institute.

——— (1999). *The way of the human, Vol. I.* Capitola, CA: Quantum Institute.

——— (1999). *The way of the human, Vol. II.* Capitola, CA: Quantum Institute.

*——— (1999). *The way of the human, Vol. III.* Capitola, CA: Quantum Institute.

*———— (2000). *I am that I am: A tribute to Sri Nisargadatta Maharaj.* Capitola, CA: Quantum Institute.

———— (2000). *Intimate relationships: Why they do and do not work.* Capitola, CA: Quantum Institute.

*———— (2002). *YOU ARE NOT: Beyond the three veils of consciousness.* Capitola, CA: Quantum Institute.

STEPHEN WOLINSKY, Ph.D., ON AUDIOTAPE

Waking from the Trance
A Practical Course on Developing Multidimensional Awareness

Sounds True presents a complete six-tape course on the tools and techniques of Quantum Psychology. Join Stephen Wolinsky as he shares detailed information on working with different dimensions of awareness, explanations of the false core/false self, and meditations to help the listener achieve a direct experience of the one substance from which all phenomena arise. Includes a discussion of Quantum Psychology's components and influences; the Advaita Vedanta tradition; Western psychological models and the terminology of quantum physics; as well as information on the life and teachings of Wolinsky's guru, Nisargadatta Maharaj.

6 cassettes in vinyl binder / 9 hours / Order #AF00521

TO ORDER, visit Sounds True on the world wide web at www.soundstrue.com or call 800-333-9185. Code SWZ1. 100% money-back guarantee.

Also Available from Your Favorite Bookstore.